Print ISBN 978-1-62385-038-8

eBook ISBN 978-1-62385-039-5

ChatGPT For Writers

Improve Your Writing in Fiction and Non-Fiction

By John Iovine

Table of Contents

Introduction

Artificial Intelligence (AI) has been used in writing programs for years. Writers are familiar with grammar checkers like Grammarly, QuillBot, ProWritingAid, and Hemingway. Recently, Generative AI has made significant strides. These newer AIs are creating a paradigm shift in writing, so much so that some writers and their unions are concerned that these AIs will render their writing skills obsolete and put them out of work.

I believe writers who are afraid to use AI will be replaced by those who do. I recommend that writers harness AI to enhance their creativity and increase their productivity.

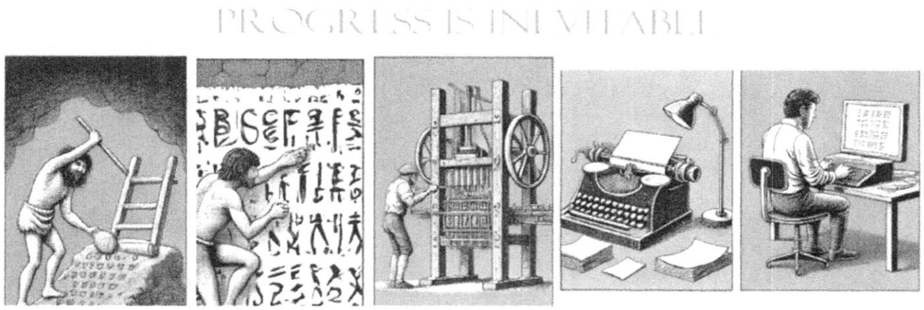

While the future of AI is limitless, AI currently performs better in some applications than others. Some AI platforms are better suited to certain applications than others. For instance, Perplexity.ai can search the internet for the latest news and research better than OpenAI's ChatGPT. That fact may change in the future, but for now, when I research internet topics, Perplexity is my go-to AI. As of this writing, OpenAI's ChatGPT can also search the internet for the latest information, as expected.

AI is Evolving

Try everything to see what works for you. Because AI continues to evolve, a task that doesn't work well today may work perfectly six months from now.

Chapter 1 – AI Assisted Writing - Copyright & IP Ownership

I utilize AI to refine and enhance my writing. I do not use AI to write my books and short stories. Although I have seen many AI instructors advocate this exact use.

For some writers, working with AI tools comes with mixed feelings. The allure of using these platforms to brainstorm, outline, or draft is undeniable; yet, they are concerned about the creative ownership of their work. Lately, the an issue of data privacy and the concern that AI has the potential to steal creative ideas. Let us look at these two issues further.

Copyright and AI-Assisted Writing

The question of whether AI-generated content can be copyrighted is currently being debated in courtrooms worldwide. These court rulings will help establish legal precedents, and new legislation may follow based on these rulings; however, for now, this is how I view the copyright status of AI-generated and AI-assisted content.

I am not a lawyer; this material on copyrights is based on my own research and opinion and should not be taken as legal advice. I believe AI-assisted writing is copyrightable.

Some Believe AI Creative Work is Not Copyrightable

The idea that AI-rendered work is not copyrightable may come from the following text in the US Government's regulations on copyright.

306 The Human Authorship Requirement

The U.S. Copyright Office will register an original work of authorship, provided that the work was created by a human being.

The copyright law only protects "the fruits of intellectual labor" that "are founded in the creative powers of the mind." *Trade-Mark Cases*, 100 U.S. 82, 94 (1879). Because copyright law is limited to "original intellectual conceptions of the author," the Office will refuse to register a claim if it determines that a human being did not create the work. *Burrow-Giles Lithographic Co. v. Sarony*, 111 U.S. 53, 58 (1884). For representative examples of works that do not satisfy this requirement, see Section 313.2 below.

Government Copyrightable Authorship

This text is on chapter 300, page 7 of the US Government's "Copyrightable Authorship: What Can Be Registered," see the link below.

https://www.copyright.gov/comp3/chap300/ch300-copyrightable-authorship.pdf

By following the strict letter of the law as stated by the US Government, the AI-rendered work can be modified by you, which invokes human authorship of the work and thus makes it copyrightable.

Modification of AI Rendered Work

Any meaningful modification of the AI-rendered work can create human authorship. Thereby making the work "AI-assisted" rather than "AI-generated." AI-assisted creative work is copyrightable.

Registered Copyrights For Me and You

Yes, you can copyright your AI-assisted content.

As a writer seeking to copyright your work, it's crucial to understand these nuances and exercise caution when incorporating AI into your creative process. To keep your creative work copyrightable, my suggestion is to use AI as your writing assistant and collaborator, and NOT as a sole content generator.

Copyright Basis

Copyright is granted automatically once your art is fixed in tangible form. This is true whether you render a piece of art, write a story, write a song, or record a piece of music. Copyright is an "automatic right." However, it is much easier to prove you are a legitimate copyright owner if you register your work with the US Government.

Why You Should Register Copyright Your Creative Work

To register your work with the US government, you will need to fill out an application, pay a filing fee, and provide a copy of the work. The copyright office will examine your application to ensure the work is eligible for copyright protection. If so, you will get an official "Certificate of Registration."

Registered copyright protection makes it easier to pursue legal recourse if anyone uses your work without your consent. If someone tries to use your creative work without permission, you can bring them to court for copyright infringement.

Is AI Stealing Your Ideas?

Another concern some writers have about using AI is that it may steal their writing ideas. Most AI platforms, including ChatGPT and Perplexity, retain user conversations for a specified period—even after a session ends. While users can often delete their conversations, it doesn't necessarily mean the data is entirely erased from the company's internal systems. In some cases, conversations may still be used in a limited way to help improve the AI model. For writers, ideas are precious, and understanding where those ideas might travel is essential.

Some of us, including myself, intentionally allow our conversations with AI to be stored. This allows me to revisit discussions and ask follow-up questions or generate new ideas from previous sessions.

How much control do we have over our ideas and data once they're in the hands of a third-party system?

Ethical AI companies have established policies to safeguard user data and intellectual property. Still, the legal landscape surrounding AI and creativity remains murky. Despite a company's best intentions, training data for these models might still contain copyrighted material or generate ideas strikingly similar to those of another user. This isn't necessarily due to malicious intent; rather, it's an inherent risk of how AI is developed.

It's also worth noting that, even if a specific conversation remains private, the AI may produce comparable ideas for other users based on patterns from its training data. For writers, this means approaching AI tools with a sense of both opportunity and caution. The benefits are considerable, but so are the potential risks to idea ownership and privacy.

Ultimately, writers must weigh the creative advantages that AI can offer against the potential impacts on their intellectual property. By understanding the issues involved, you can make an informed decision to use (or not use) AI as a creative partner. Personally, I am not concerned about my AI conversation being used as training data.

Chapter 2- AI is a Writer's Toolbox

AI can augment and amplify your personal and business writing skills. In many ways, AI surpasses the definition of a tool and may be thought of as a partner and collaborator.

Fiction Writing:
AI will supercharge your writing process. AI can help generate ideas, plots, plot twists, and characters, and rephrase and rewrite text to improve your writing.

Non-Fiction Writing:
AI can do everything mentioned above, plus assist in developing non-fiction ideas, creating outlines, summarizing text, conducting research, and performing reference lookups.

Business Writing & Reports
AI can assist in generating business reports from data and writing company emails and product sales copy.

Blogs
Blogs and article writing become so much easier when you have an AI to assist you with writing and researching.

Vision OCR and Reading Charts
AI Vision's capabilities enable it to read and interpret charts and financial reports. It can summarize articles, read legal documents, and help you interpret the text. See Chapter 14.

Psychology and Character Development
You can bounce personal feelings and characters' interpersonal relationships to the AI for feedback.

AI is so competent in psychology that shortly, I expect AI to augment human therapists or become competent clinical social workers themselves. Humans may trust their AI therapist more than their human counterparts.

Putting this aspect of AI will improve your characters' realism and motivation.

Book Contracts & Legal Documents
AI is not a lawyer but can easily pass any bar exam. It can be used to read and explain legal documents and terminology. AI can provide insight into copyright, licenses, book, and article contracts.

It can also write simple legal documents. The boilerplate photography releases available online were too bulky and detailed for my simple transaction. So, I asked my AI to write a photograph release. In the first round, the AI gave me a three-page release. That was still too much legalize. I asked the AI to reduce it to one page. It performed and gave me the bare-bones release I needed with the extra-legal verbiage.

Poems, Song & Music Writing

AI can write poetry, songs, and music. I don't expect a Grammy winner to thank his AI for his hit song, but that doesn't mean it hasn't happened.

Translation

Provide your AI with text, and the AI can translate that text into any number of languages or translate foreign languages into English.

Writing Tutor

The AI can tutor you in many subjects, including English. AI can act like a grammar checker, thesaurus, and dictionary, and offer word alternatives.

Problem Solving - Working with Hemingway

If you have a thorny plot problem or writing issue, you can work it through with the AI acting like one of your favorite or famous writers. Imagine working with a Hemingway AI or Fitzgerald AI on a plot point.

Research

The latest iteration of AIs has access to the Internet. This means they can assist you with research and historical information.

Everyday Miscellaneous Issues

I turn to AI to help me solve minor issues. In the last few days, I have asked it how to add a heart to an iPhone text message, explain the difference between the hot, common, and ground in a home AC power system, draw a simple op-amp amplifier using a 741 op-amp, and generate a text-to-art prompt based on a picture I uploaded to the AI. The AI helped me troubleshoot unlocking the screen rotation on my iPad.

What more would you want from a writing assistant?

Remember, AI can be many things; it can be a tool, your assistant, and your collaborator.

Copyrights - Authenticity of Originality
This question was answered in Chapter 1.

Most writers are already using AI augmentation. Sophisticated writing tools, like Grammarly, Quill Bot, and spell checkers, use AI. I believe that when AI is used as a tool rather than a content creator, you remain the creator, and your work remains authentic to you and copyrightable.

GPT50 is one of Many

GPT is the acronym for "Generative Pre-trained Transformer." This language model has been trained on a large amount of text (deep learning) to produce results that mimic human writing. When you add the word "Chat" to GPT, you get "ChatGPT," which is a chatbot.

There are many AI platforms on the market. ChatGPT from OpenAI is one of the most recognizable; it may not be the best in every application.

GPT50 is a powerful AI tool that will help you create great content. In this book, I will demonstrate with examples how to use these AIs effectively.

Chapter 3 -Opening an AI Account

You have many options when it comes to choosing an AI. I will use OpenAI as a primary example. Near the end of the chapter, alternative AI's are listed.

Signing Up for ChatGPT

Go to: https://chat.openai.com

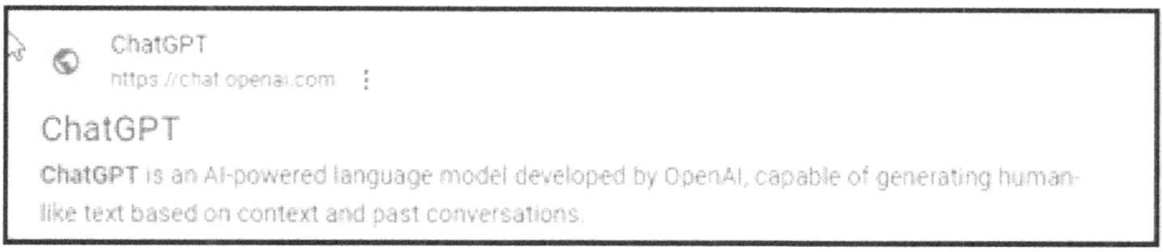

Register for an account using your email address and create a password; refer to the image below.

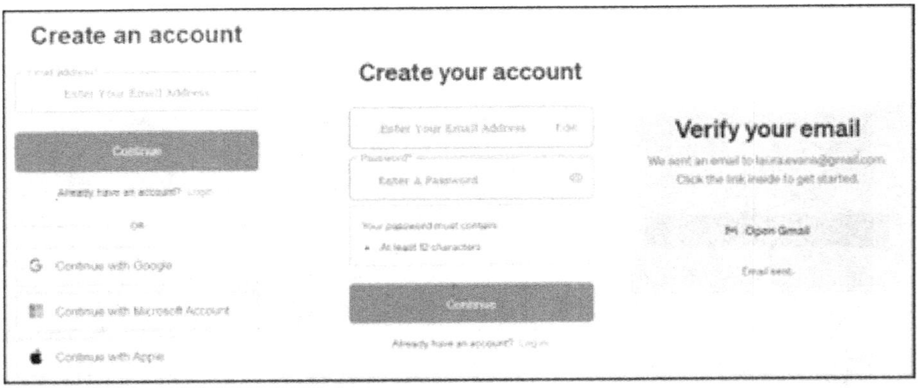

You can use ChatGPT5 for free, which is the best way to start. When ready, you can upgrade to ChatGPT5 for $20.00 per month. At this subscription level, you have access to GPT5o (omni), a higher-level AI model with better creativity.

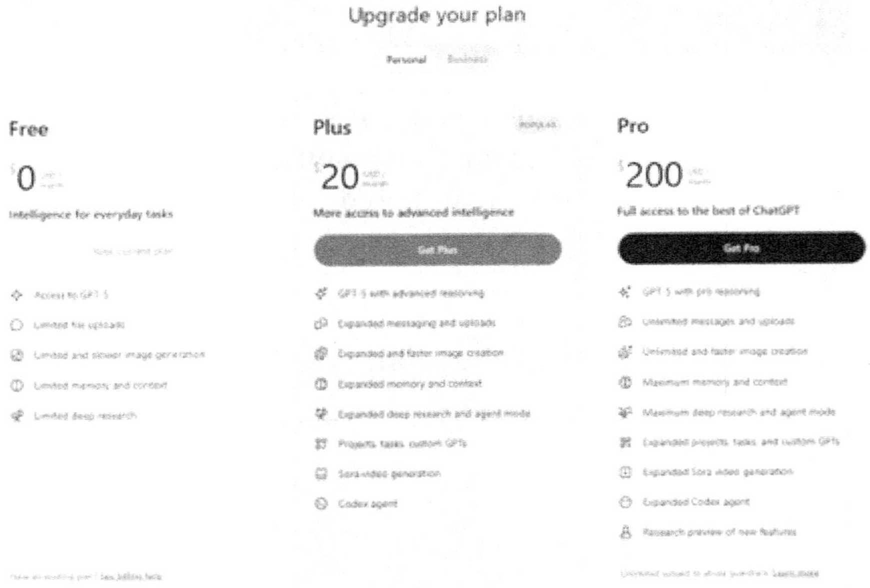

Once your account is created and your email verified, you can access the ChatGPT AI.

If you upgrade from the free versions, new iterations of ChatGPT will be made available to you when they are developed.

More AI Bots

OpenAI's ChatGPT is probably the most familiar of the Chatbots, but numerous alternatives exist. Most AI bots have similar sign-on procedures and typically have a free version for people to try.

Twitter X Grok

Grok.ai is available to premium members of Twitter X. This free with X subscription is limited. Access is restricted to five queries every 12 hours. As of this writing, the monthly subscription cost for SuperGrok is $30.00. Grok's unique advantage lies in its ability to provide unbiased information on politically charged topics, such as climate change, immigration, and green energy costs, without being influenced by politically correct thinking. This gives users a more objective and factual perspective on these issues, fostering a more informed and open dialogue.

Perplexity

The free version of Perplexity.ai can be accessed here.

https://www.perplexity.ai/

The pro version costs $20.00 per month.

What is exceptional about this AI, is that it does an extensive web search to answer the question. It provides the reference URLs to its answer. AIs are incorporating web searches to provide access to up-to-date information.

AI Aggregators - Futurepedia, Gmtech, Magai, Edenai

The One Service To Include Them All

There are AI aggregator services that allow their users to access and utilize a wide variety of LLMs and Image Generators for a single monthly cost.

Basic services start at $14.99 per month. Accessing an AI costs a fraction of a cent, typically around $0.01 per AI response. Each service has its unique plan. You will need to visit the AI site to obtain its details.

This money is deducted from your credits. Additional credits can be purchased if you exceed your $5.00 monthly allocation.

https://gmtech.com/

Below is a screenshot of their current AI integrations.

All Models can be viewed here:
https://app.gmtech.com/model_status/
To reach Magai
https://magai.co/

Magai provides access to over 50 large language models and more than 5 AI image models.

To reach Futurepedia:
https://www.futurepedia.io/

To reach Eden AI:
https://www.edenai.co/

You may want to explore new AI aggregators, as more services emerge all the time. These services provide users with access to various AI platforms for a single monthly price.

Chapter 4 - Crafting Prompts

Using AI effectively involves crafting prompts that communicate with the AI in a manner that yields your desired results.

This book will guide you in crafting effective writing prompts. Writing prompts for financial analysis, physics, and astronomy would require a different methodology than what is outline here.

Crafting effective prompts is a skill that can be learned.

Prompts

I don't think anyone would argue that crafting prompts is the key to unleashing the power of AI.

Creating The Perfect Prompt

There's no such thing as a perfect prompt. However, I can offer a mindset and framework for prompts that will save you a significant amount of time.

One - Don't think in terms of prompts as a singular question; think in terms of conversations. You don't need to fit your inquiry in a single sentence or paragraph. Instead of a multi-question approach modal prompt, think in single chained prompts. An example of this will clarify.

Suppose you write Paranormal fiction, and you want to try to determine the audience for your book and how to reach your readers through advertising.

You don't need to combine both questions into a single prompt. In fact, it would be better to split up these questions. And think of each question as part of an ongoing conversation. The entire chat can be stored and revisited whenever you want to continue that "conversation".

Two - Assign a persona to the AI. If you are looking to develop marketing strategies or materials for your new book, consider assigning a persona to an AI.

Example 1 -Need a Book Sales and Marketing Expert. Have a famous marketer in mind, such as Seth Godin; name them "for style" in your marketing prompt.

Example 2 - Imagine you're writing a fiction novel. You need information for your character to extract a bullet from your heroine. Assign the AI the persona of a medical doctor who specializes in trauma.

Three - Tell the AI to ask you any clarifying questions it may have to generate the best response possible to your inquiry or prompt. With this mindset and framework, you are ready to use AI to tackle any problem.

You can use ChatGPT to do any of the following:

1 - Generate book ideas based on a topic.
2 - Generate fiction book outlines.
3 - Generate book titles.
4 - Summarize text
5 - Rewrite and improve text.
6 - Help create book characters.
7 - Generate non-fiction outlines (solar, wind, etc.)
8 - Generate character descriptions.
9 - Generate pros and cons of decisions or ideas.
10 - Generate lists.
11 - Generate poems
12 – Generate songs
13 – Critique and give feedback on your story/text.
14 – Help describing police or medical procedures, etc.
15 - Language translations
16 - Generate prompts for Text to Art AI.
17 - Personal Instructor for learning
18 - Write emails – personal and business
19 - Craft response – business and personal
20 - Act as a tutor when taking online learning classes
21 - Offer insight into your character's behavior.

The above list is only a fraction of AI capabilities. Many of the prompts we touch upon in this chapter are explored in greater detail in the following chapters.

Prompts - Open, Fixed, and Conversations

Open - Open prompts allow the AI to generate the most creative responses. For example, "Write 300 words on the advantages of Solar Energy." The topic can vary, such as the best foods for diabetics or diets.

ChatGPT did an excellent job writing 300 words on the advantages of solar energy.

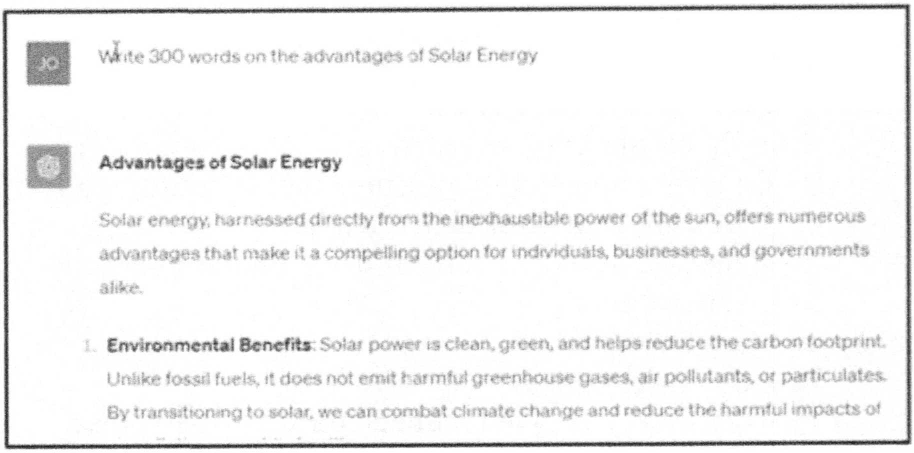

Fixed - This prompt asks for a specific fact or facts. For example, "Who was the third President of the United States?" Keep in mind that the AI can hallucinate facts and data, so remember to double-check its data output.

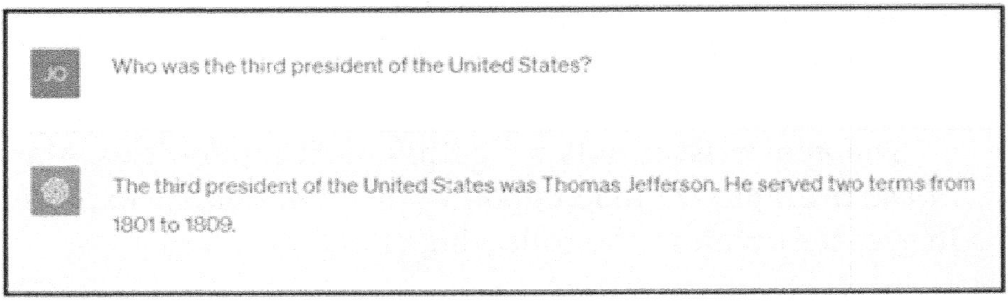

Chat - Creating a character response with ChatGPT. In this scenario, my 13-year-old character, Tommy, has a problem explaining to his dad, a doctor, why he failed a biology test. I asked ChatGPT to provide me with a few ideas on how a character might respond to a dilemma. ChatGPT provided six possible options.

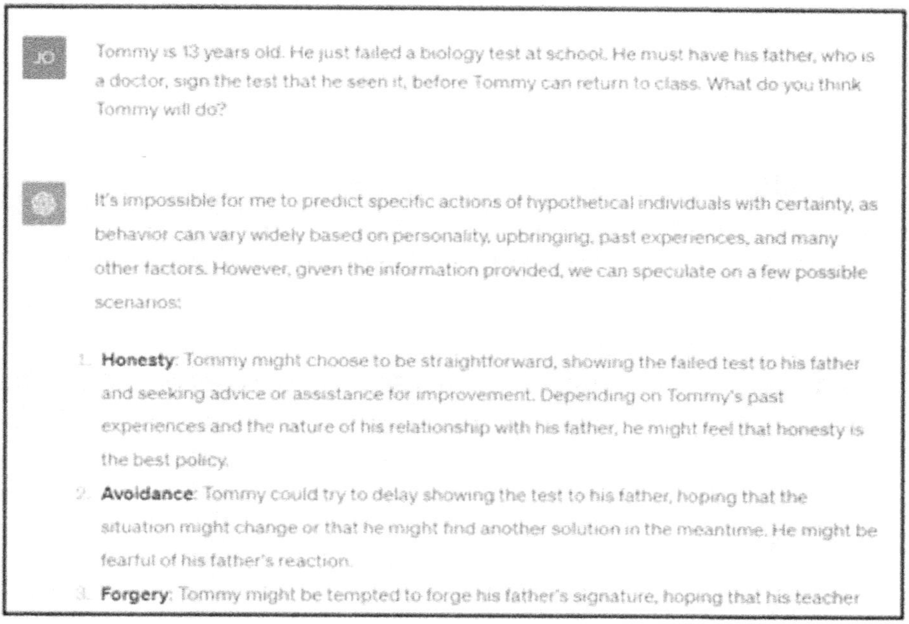
JO

Tommy is 13 years old. He just failed a biology test at school. He must have his father, who is a doctor, sign the test that he seen it, before Tommy can return to class. What do you think Tommy will do?

It's impossible for me to predict specific actions of hypothetical individuals with certainty, as behavior can vary widely based on personality, upbringing, past experiences, and many other factors. However, given the information provided, we can speculate on a few possible scenarios:

1. **Honesty**: Tommy might choose to be straightforward, showing the failed test to his father and seeking advice or assistance for improvement. Depending on Tommy's past experiences and the nature of his relationship with his father, he might feel that honesty is the best policy.
2. **Avoidance**: Tommy could try to delay showing the test to his father, hoping that the situation might change or that he might find another solution in the meantime. He might be fearful of his father's reaction.
3. **Forgery**: Tommy might be tempted to forge his father's signature, hoping that his teacher

Jumping Off From Any Branch

You can use any one of those AI response ideas as a jumping-off point, or those suggestions could even trigger your imagination for a completely different response you may want to pursue.

Remember It's Not Just One (Bite of the Apple) Prompt

I see many people writing prompts and ending the inquiry with AI after one prompt. No. You can continue to ask and refine your question, drilling down until you are satisfied with the answer.

In the above "Tommy" example, suppose you wanted to pursue the "Avoidance" scenario. You could ask the AI to fill out the idea with the potential consequences for Tommy for taking this action.

If the AI's response is too vague, drill down with additional prompts asking for greater detail.

Talk To Me, Formal - Informal

You can direct the AI to write responses in a formal, academic manner.

Alternatively, you can ask the AI to respond in a friendly and informal manner. I would shy away from AI jokes and AI sarcasm. The last time I checked, the AI hadn't evolved to the point where that could be pulled off credibly.

Positive and Confident

I like my AI to be positive and confident. But I wouldn't want to ask my AI to be "Positive & Confident" at the beginning of every conversation. Here is where you can implement GPTs.

I devoted a full chapter to how to create GPTs and what they are. Think of them as a procedural script saved to the OpenAI server, which you can call at any time.

In general, the quality of the AI's response is proportional to the quality of your prompts. The following are a bunch of quick-start tips for writing effective prompts. Many of these tips have full chapters devoted to exploring their use.

Segmenting AI's Large Knowledge Base

The AI has a vast and extensive knowledge database. We can obtain better responses by instructing the AI to segment its knowledge into an area of interest to us. This is the reason we ask the AI to assume a persona. Many prompts of this type begin with the famous "As an expert [you name the topic].

Establish Your Audience

The AI will generate better responses if it understands its audience. Explaining a medical issue to an adolescent is different from explaining it to an adult and different from explaining it to other medical professionals.

Establishing the AI's Tonality

We touched upon this before. Do we want the AI to respond in a neutral, formal, informal, friendly, and confident manner?

Background

Providing the AI with specific settings will enhance its response. Imagine the difference in a marine's response when fighting in a jungle, an urban city, or a spaceport 50 light-years from Earth.

By incorporating this information into your prompt, the AI's response will be focused and on target.

Wash, Rinse, and Repeat

Save your best prompts. You can use software like Evernote to create a library of prompts.

Editing

The following two chapters will highlight prompts for fiction and nonfiction writing. The AI is a great editor. It can do basic checks for grammar, spelling, and typos. But it can do much more. The following prompts are a few you can use for editing.

Quick Start Prompts for Editing

Use these short, focused prompts to refine, tighten, or reshape your writing. Each one helps improve clarity, tone, or structure when editing existing text.

Editing Goal	AI Prompt Example
Polish	"Refine the following paragraph for clarity and rhythm. Remove filler, smooth awkward phrasing, and tighten the prose."
Summarize	"Condense the following text into a short summary that captures all key ideas and preserves the original meaning."
Organize Notes	"Turn these scattered or unstructured notes into a logical outline with clear sections, order, and flow."
Adjust Tone	"Rewrite this passage in a [tone: journalistic, conversational, professional, empathetic, or neutral] style while keeping the facts accurate."
Clarify & Connect	"Edit the following text to improve clarity and transitions. Ensure each sentence flows naturally into the next."

Chapter 5- Writing Fiction: Story, Plot and Characters

Fiction - Story Plot and Outline

If you have an idea for a story or don't, you can ask AI to fill in a story plot and outline.

Let's start with the first scenario: You have an idea you want to develop and move forward with. The following is an idea I have for a science fiction story that I plan to write.

A group of astronauts orbiting the Earth sees it suddenly disappear. However, the Earth's clouds are still present, and the space station and moon are still held in orbit around the missing planet. One astronaut recalled reading about an experiment at CERN aimed at creating a subatomic black hole. The astronauts surmised that the black hole was made and swallowed the Earth. Their only hope is to break orbit and reach Mars, where supplies are waiting to establish a small colony.

I added the following directive at the beginning of my idea. Write a plot and story outline for the following science fiction novel.

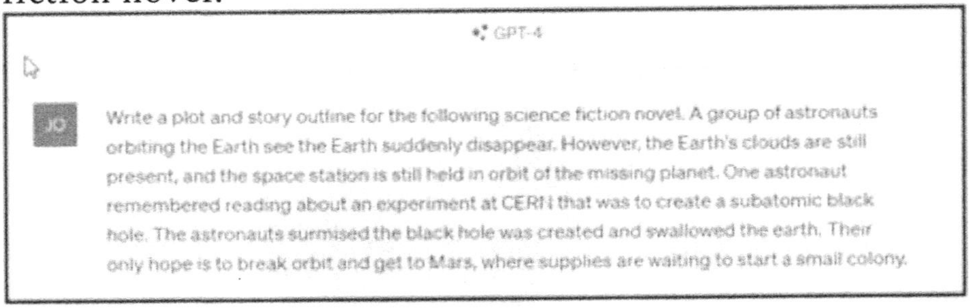

These original prompts were sent with ChatGPT4. ChatGPT 5 is an advance model and will provide better responses than outline here. Next, I sent my request and idea to ChatGPT4, and I obtained three parts plus an epilogue. Part 1 is shown below.

Title: *Whispers in the Void*

Part I: The Vanishing

1. **The Unfathomable View:** Aboard the space station, astronauts are going about their daily tasks when one of them notices a peculiar sight: the Earth is gone. Panic sets in as they try to contact ground control, but there's only silence. The Earth's clouds are eerily floating, suggesting the planet is still there but invisible.
2. **Denial and Realization:** The astronauts discuss various theories for the sudden disappearance. Perhaps it's a technological glitch in the space station's system? Or a massive cloaking device? As they're brainstorming, an astronaut named Michael recalls an article about CERN's experiment.
3. **Michael's Revelation:** Michael explains the concept of subatomic black holes and theorizes that if one was created, it might have swallowed Earth from the inside out, leaving only the outermost atmospheric layers behind.
4. **The Impact:** While grappling with the potential loss of their families and homes, the astronauts have to face the immediate reality of dwindling supplies.

The AI provided a title for the book, "Whispers in the Void," that I consider an OK working title. Part 1 closely follows my thoughts. Let's move on to part 2.

Part II: A Hope Beyond

1. **The Plan:** With limited time and resources, the astronauts decide their best chance for survival is to break orbit and head to Mars.
2. **The Hurdles:** Leaving the space station is tricky; it wasn't designed for long-distance travel. The astronauts have to improvise solutions, deal with system failures, and overcome their personal conflicts and fears.
3. **The First Glimpse:** As they approach Mars, they discover that communication channels with the Mars base are also silent. Panic ensues as they question if the black hole phenomenon affected more than just Earth.
4. **Descent into Unknown:** Landing on Mars, they find the base deserted. However, there's evidence of recent habitation, indicating the colony might have relocated or be temporarily away.

The first two plot points in part 2 align with my thinking. However, plot points 3 and 4 are not. I think there are only supplies on Mars waiting in anticipation for colonists to arrive. Let's continue to part 3.

Part III: New Beginnings

1. **Traces of Humanity:** Searching the base, the astronauts find logs that hint at a subterranean refuge.
2. **The Descent:** Following the clues, they discover an underground city with survivors from Mars, as well as a few from Earth who had been visiting Mars during the incident. It turns out the base had been compromised by unexpected atmospheric changes, forcing the inhabitants to move underground.
3. **The Unified Goal:** With combined resources and knowledge, the united group of survivors begin the monumental task of establishing a sustainable colony on Mars.
4. **Echoes from Earth:** As the days turn into months, an odd phenomenon occurs. Strange, ghost-like echoes of radio signals from Earth begin to reach Mars. The signals are old broadcasts, songs, news reports - a nostalgic reminder of the lost planet. It gives the survivors hope that Earth might still be there in some form, waiting to be rediscovered.

In part 3, the deviation from my original thoughts for this story continues. If this were an active project, I could massage my original prompt to adhere more closely to my ideas. Or I could incorporate the randomness of the AI plot points. Read plot point 4, Echos from Earth. This would certainly be a twist after thinking everyone on Earth was dead for most of the story.

Now, we move on to the final part, the Epilogue.

Epilogue:

Several years later, a new generation, born on Mars, looks up at the sky. They've grown up hearing tales of the blue planet that once was. A new mission is proposed, with the aim of venturing back to where Earth once was, to uncover its mysteries and to seek answers to the enigmatic event that led to humanity's great migration. The legacy of Earth lives on in stories, hopes, and aspirations of its descendants on Mars.

I am not thrilled with the Epilogue, but if this were an active project, the epilogue could be developed.

Second Scenario - I don't know what I want to write next.

You have succumbed to writer's block. You want to write a science fiction story, but don't have an idea. You can ask the AI to come up with ten ideas for a science fiction story, or you can choose a topic yourself.

First, we have the AI generate ten ideas.

JO

List 10 ideas for a science fiction story.

1. **The Memory Market:** In a future where memories can be traded, bought, or stolen, a detective investigates a black market that deals in the rarest and most dangerous memories, only to discover one of his own memories being auctioned off.
2. **Parallel Paradox:** An engineer accidentally creates a portal to parallel universes. Each universe represents a different outcome from every decision she's ever made. As she jumps from one to another, she loses track of her original world and must decide where she truly belongs.
3. **Digital Afterlife:** After death, people's consciousnesses are uploaded to a virtual reality. A young woman discovers a plot to corrupt and control these digital souls and teams up with a group of hackers to prevent a digital apocalypse.
4. **Solar Sailing Pirates:** In a galaxy where ships sail on solar winds, a fearsome band of pirates is pursued by a determined admiral. However, as they duel across stars, they unearth ancient cosmic secrets that might reshape their universe.

5. **Alien Anthropologists:** Earth is actually a zoo/experiment set up by advanced aliens. When the experiment ends, they plan to reset Earth, wiping out humanity. A group of humans stumbles upon this secret and tries to negotiate for their species' survival.
6. **Last Robot Standing:** In a post-apocalyptic world where humans have perished, a lone robot continues its programmed task: to take care of a city and its non-existent inhabitants. Over time, it starts to develop emotions and a longing for companionship.
7. **The Time Capsule:** A device is discovered that lets people send objects back in time, but not forward. Societies and economies collapse as everyone becomes obsessed with correcting their pasts. A group seeks to destroy the device, but are constantly thwarted by their past selves.
8. **Galactic Gardeners:** Plant-based aliens arrive at a barren Earth, finding humanity extinct due to environmental collapse. They decide to terraform Earth, planting trees and forests that have strange and mystical properties, but in doing so, accidentally revive the last surviving human cryogenically frozen.
9. **Mindscape Architects:** In a society where dreams can be designed and shared, "Dream Architects" are the most sought-after professionals. When a series of shared nightmares begins to terrorize the populace, a rookie architect and a seasoned detective must team up to find the source.
10. **The Silence Spectrum:** People on Earth suddenly gain the ability to perceive a new color, one that's otherworldly and beautiful. With it comes a silent frequency. Those who become obsessed with this new hue begin to change, developing strange abilities and an alien mindset, leading to societal rifts and fear of the unknown.

You can run with any of those ideas or use your own. Let's run with the first idea generated by the AI. Let's add my directive sentence, Write a plot and story outline for the following science fiction novel, to the beginning of the idea.

JO

Write a plot and story outline for the following science fiction novel. The Memory Market: In a future where memories can be traded, bought, or stolen, a detective investigates a black market that deals in the rarest and most dangerous memories, only to discover one of his own memories being auctioned off.

Title: *Echoes of the Past*

Part I: The Memory Economy

1. **The Future Landscape**: The story is set in a sprawling metropolis in the year 2145. Advanced neural technology allows memories to be extracted, stored, and implanted into other individuals. Legally, these memory exchanges serve purposes such as entertainment, therapy, or education.
2. **Detective Alan Rourke**: Our protagonist is a grizzled detective with a storied past. He's seen the best and worst of humanity, and the memory trade has always rubbed him the wrong way. Yet, he's benefited from it too, using "experience packs" to rapidly gain skills.
3. **The First Case**: Rourke is called to investigate a theft where the victim had a memory stolen without their consent. This isn't new, but the nature of the memory - a seemingly innocuous day at a park - piques his interest.

Again, the AI has created a suitable title, background, and protagonist. Moving on to part 2.

Part II: Into the Shadows

1. **The Black Market's Allure**: Rourke dives deep into the city's underbelly, uncovering the existence of the memory black market. Here, memories are not just traded for leisure or education but for power, manipulation, and blackmail.
2. **Dangerous Memories**: Rourke discovers that certain memories, especially those filled with adrenaline or intense emotion, are highly addictive. Some people have become "Memory Junkies," constantly chasing the high of extreme experiences without living them.
3. **Personal Stakes**: While undercover, Rourke attends a black market auction. He's horrified to see a memory of his own up for sale - a deeply personal moment with a loved one he lost years ago. He's tormented by the idea of strangers viewing his most intimate memories.

The AI provides excellent plot points and development, on to part 3.

Part III: Revelations

1. **The Hunt for Answers**: Consumed by anger and betrayal, Rourke seeks to uncover who stole his memory and why. Along the way, he discovers a vast web of intrigue, where memories serve as currency for the elite and powerful to control the masses.
2. **The Twisted Mogul**: At the heart of the conspiracy is a tech mogul, Elara Vance, who has discovered a way to manipulate memories, not just view them. Her goal: to rewrite history in her favor and use collective memories to control societal narratives.
3. **The Showdown**: As Rourke confronts Vance, he's faced with a choice - reclaim his stolen memory and let Vance go or sacrifice his past to bring down the memory market for good.

The AI develops the plot, beginning with a personal issue for the protagonist and progressing to a global issue for the world in part 4.

Part IV: A New Dawn

1. **The Collapse**: With Vance's empire crumbling, the memory market undergoes strict regulation. Memory transfers still occur, but the black market's unchecked power has been curtailed.
2. **Rourke's Choice**: In the end, Rourke decides not to reclaim his stolen memory. He realizes that while memories shape us, it's the lessons we take from them and the choices we make that truly define us.
3. **Epilogue**: Rourke leaves the city, setting off into the unknown with a fresh perspective on life, understanding that memories are sacred, personal experiences that shouldn't be commodified or manipulated.

Throughout the novel, themes of privacy, the essence of identity, the dangers of unchecked technology, and the value of experiences resonate strongly, prompting readers to reflect on their own memories and the weight they hold in their lives.

A complete story outline. Remember, every section and plot point can be tweaked to align with your vision and sensibilities.

Chapter 6 - Writing Non-Fiction; ideas, outline, etc.

Non-Fiction Work

If you are using AI to assist in writing non-fiction material, be careful. AI can sometimes “hallucinate” information, providing inaccurate or fabricated information in such great detail that you would unquestioningly consider it true.

When researching a medical topic, I have encountered an AI that completely fabricates medical facts, including fake citations to non-existent studies and papers, and provides fictional, non-working URLs. I was stunned by the details involved in the fabrication by the AI.

Unfortunately, we often tend to believe computers and AI when they quote facts. Always verify any facts generated by AI. With AI, trust but verify.

To make "trust but verify" a repeatable process, use this quick checklist whenever you rely on AI-generated information:

1. Require source URLs in outputs.
   Always ask the AI to provide direct source links for any factual claims or statistics.
2. Open and skim each source.
   Don't trust the headline or summary alone – open the link, scroll through the article, and confirm the key point actually matches the AI's statement.
3. Cross-check with a second source.
   Look for another credible source (e.g., government, university, or peer-reviewed journal) to confirm the claim.
4. Flag "no-source claims" for manual review.
   If the AI can't provide a source, mark that item as "unverified" until you find confirmation yourself.
5. Save verified citations to a reference manager.
   Use apps like Evernote to keep a searchable archive of your confirmed references for future writing.

Reducing AI Hallucinations

You can improve accuracy by using a few simple techniques:

- **Copy and paste exact paper titles or URLs** into your prompt. This anchors the AI to real studies instead of generating approximate citations.
- **Use advanced search syntax:** try *site:gov*, *site:edu*, or *site:nih.gov* to focus results on authoritative domains.

- **Upload PDFs and ask the AI to quote directly** with page numbers — this ensures transparency and helps you trace each fact back to its source.

Plagiarism

AI tools are designed not to copy existing content verbatim; it's wise to run AI-generated text through a plagiarism checker as a precaution.

Non-Fiction Idea and Outline

You can direct an AI to develop ideas and outlines if you have an idea for a nonfiction article or book. You can also direct the AI to provide ideas if you are stuck for inspiration.

Let's start with the first scenario: You have an idea you want to develop and move forward with. The following is an idea I have for personal development that I plan on writing about.

While many self-help how-to development articles/books focus on goal setting, my article will be specifically on perseverance toward a goal. When a person initially sets a goal, the excitement and the plans to achieve it drive them forward. Most worthwhile goals take a considerable amount of time to achieve. My book is about how to persevere and keep grinding toward your goal when your enthusiasm wanes, and you're tempted to stop and pursue a different, brighter, and shinier goal.

I added the following directive at the beginning of my idea. Rewrite and improve this idea as a directive to develop this idea into an outline for writing.

> JO
>
> Rewrite and improve this idea as a directive to develop this idea into an outline for writing.
>
> While many self-help how-to development articles/books focus on goal setting, my article will be specifically on perseverance toward a goal. When a person initially sets a goal, the excitement of setting a goal and the plans to achieve drive you forward. Most worthwhile goals take a considerable amount of time to achieve. So my article is about how to persevere and keep grinding toward your goal when your enthusiasm dissipates and you prefer to stop and pursue a different bright and shiny goal.

The AI responds with a title and objective.

> **Directive for Developing an Article Outline:**
>
> **Title:** *Staying the Course: Nurturing Perseverance in Long-Term Goal Achievement*
>
> **Objective:**
> To craft a comprehensive guide that emphasizes the importance of perseverance in goal achievement, especially when initial enthusiasm wanes. The article will provide actionable steps and strategies to help readers maintain focus and drive, even when tempted by newer, seemingly more appealing goals.

Followed by a 7-chapter outline, with sub-points to hit inside each chapter.

Article Outline:

1. **Introduction:**
   - Briefly discuss the universal allure of setting new goals.
   - Highlight the common challenge: sustaining momentum after the initial excitement fades.
2. **The Psychology of New Goals:**
   - Delve into why we're attracted to new goals.
   - Discuss the dopamine release when embarking on a new venture and its eventual reduction.
3. **The Pitfalls of Goal-Hopping:**
   - Discuss the consequences of abandoning goals mid-way.
   - Highlight the cycle of perpetual dissatisfaction and lack of achievement.
4. **Strategies to Cultivate Perseverance:**
   - **Remembering Your 'Why':** Reconnect with the reason you set the goal in the first place.
   - **Milestones and Celebrations:** Break the goal down into smaller tasks and celebrate small victories.
   - **Visualization:** Regularly visualize the end result and the emotions attached to the achievement.
   - **Accountability Partners:** Share your goal with someone who can provide motivation and check-ins.
   - **Re-Evaluation:** Periodically assess if the goal still aligns with your values and long-term objectives.
   - **Growth Mindset:** Embrace challenges and setbacks as opportunities for growth.
5. **Tales of Triumph:**
   - Share real-life stories or anecdotes of individuals who achieved significant goals by demonstrating persistence and dedication.
6. **Addressing the Lure of the 'Shiny New Goal':**
   - Strategies to differentiate between genuine new passions and fleeting distractions.
   - Encouraging a balance between pursuing new interests without sacrificing primary goals.
7. **Conclusion:**
   - Reiterate the value of perseverance in achieving lasting satisfaction and success.
   - Encourage readers to commit to their goals, using the provided strategies as a guide.

It ends its response with a note to the writer.

Note to Writer:

Ensure that the article is enriched with data, quotations, and expert opinions where relevant. Engage readers with questions, encouraging self-reflection on their own goal-setting and pursuit behaviors.

Greater focus

I could get the AI to achieve greater focus by defining a personality to imitate and an audience. I am not doing that here. Let's assume you are happy with this outline; one way you could proceed is to ask the AI to write on each point.

The first point in Chapter 1, Introduction, is to briefly discuss the universal allure of setting new goals.

You could begin fleshing out the document by asking the AI to write 100 words on that first point.

Write 100 words - briefly discuss the universal allure of setting new goals.

ChatGPT responds with:

Write 100 words - briefly discuss the universal allure of setting new goals.

Setting new goals is universally alluring because it taps into our innate desire for growth, progress, and purpose. When we establish a fresh objective, we invigorate our sense of direction and reignite passion. Goals offer a tangible future vision, a brighter prospect that we can strive towards. This act of looking forward brings with it a surge of motivation and optimism. In essence, setting new goals becomes a symbolic act of self-renewal, allowing us to reimagine our potential and recommit to our aspirations. It's a testament to our belief in endless possibilities and our capability to evolve.

You can continue in this manner until you have a complete article ready for editing.

Idea Generation

If you don't have a clear-cut topic for your article/book, you can ask the AI to create ideas for you. Using the idea of required perseverance toward a goal, we can ask the AI the following.

Please generate five self-help article ideas that focus on the how-to of maintaining perseverance in achieving a goal.

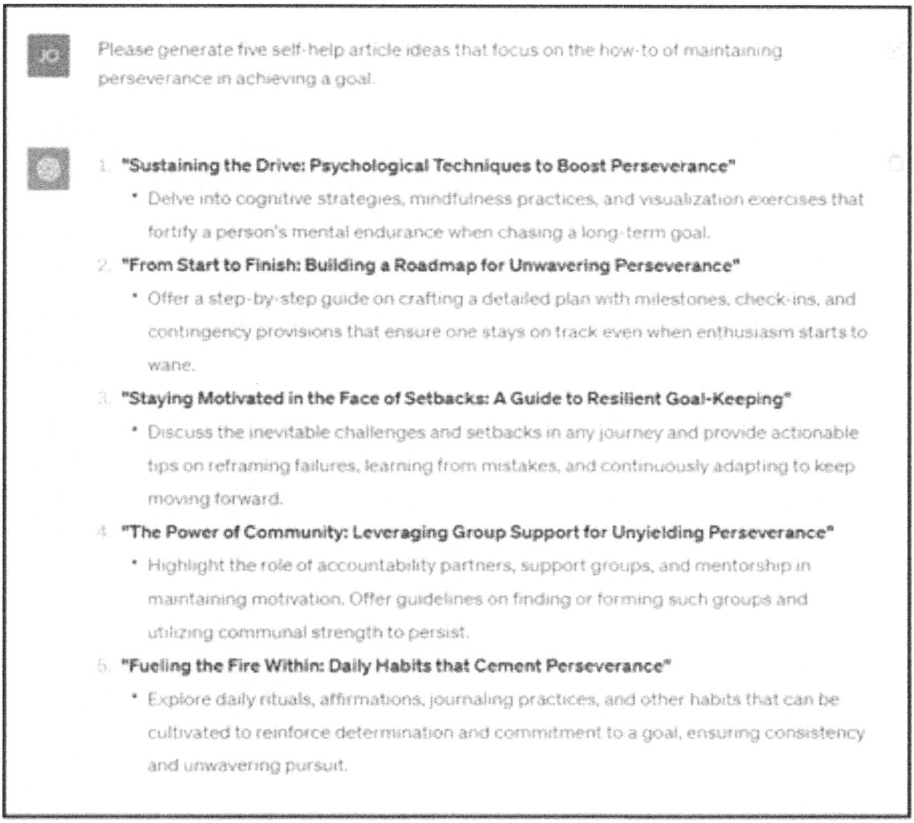
JO

Please generate five self-help article ideas that focus on the how-to of maintaining perseverance in achieving a goal.

1. **"Sustaining the Drive: Psychological Techniques to Boost Perseverance"**
   - Delve into cognitive strategies, mindfulness practices, and visualization exercises that fortify a person's mental endurance when chasing a long-term goal.
2. **"From Start to Finish: Building a Roadmap for Unwavering Perseverance"**
   - Offer a step-by-step guide on crafting a detailed plan with milestones, check-ins, and contingency provisions that ensure one stays on track even when enthusiasm starts to wane.
3. **"Staying Motivated in the Face of Setbacks: A Guide to Resilient Goal-Keeping"**
   - Discuss the inevitable challenges and setbacks in any journey and provide actionable tips on reframing failures, learning from mistakes, and continuously adapting to keep moving forward.
4. **"The Power of Community: Leveraging Group Support for Unyielding Perseverance"**
   - Highlight the role of accountability partners, support groups, and mentorship in maintaining motivation. Offer guidelines on finding or forming such groups and utilizing communal strength to persist.
5. **"Fueling the Fire Within: Daily Habits that Cement Perseverance"**
   - Explore daily rituals, affirmations, journaling practices, and other habits that can be cultivated to reinforce determination and commitment to a goal, ensuring consistency and unwavering pursuit.

Each article idea provided by the AI can be drilled down as we did with the first idea.

Chapter 7 - Sudowrite For Topics AI Will Not Write

There are many things that our standard AI platforms will refuse to write. In the case of ChatGPT, any content outside OpenAI's Content Guidelines will be rejected or throttled back.

These include too graphic scenes of violence, sex, rape, incest, or slavery. I can't list everything that could trigger a content warning or dismissal of services, but in the middle of writing a novel, you don't want to argue with your AI writing assistant.

Sudowrite will assist you in writing when other platforms refuse your request. Sudowrite is an AI designed to assist writers in writing creative fiction. Like other AIs, Sudowrite is intended to assist you in your writing, not to do the writing for you.

Sudowrite is powerful, and I believe it is slightly better than general-purpose AIs for writing fiction. However, for non-fiction writing, I feel GPT5o is the stronger AI.

That said, let's examine a few of Sudowrite's features for fiction. The following is the stock Sudowrite home screen.

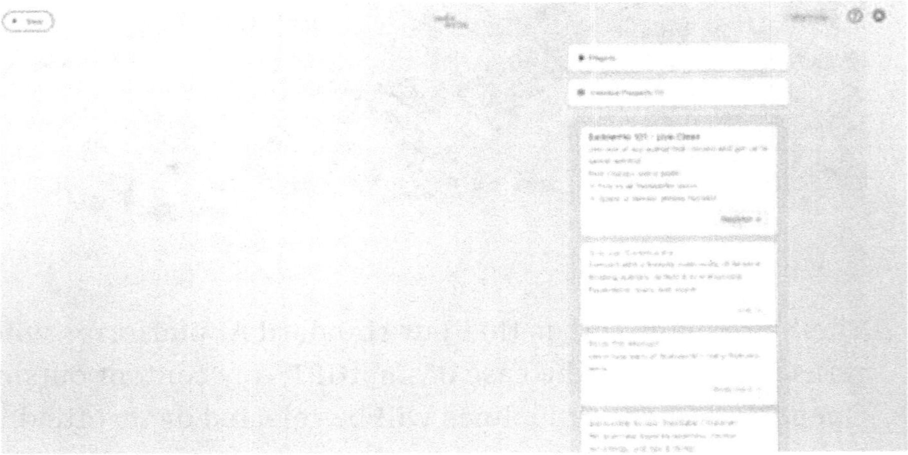

Please note that this is a brief overview of Sudowrite. To explore all of its features, a book would be required. However, beginners can utilize Sudowrite at its elementary levels and still derive excellent results.

This is my home screen of Sudowrite.

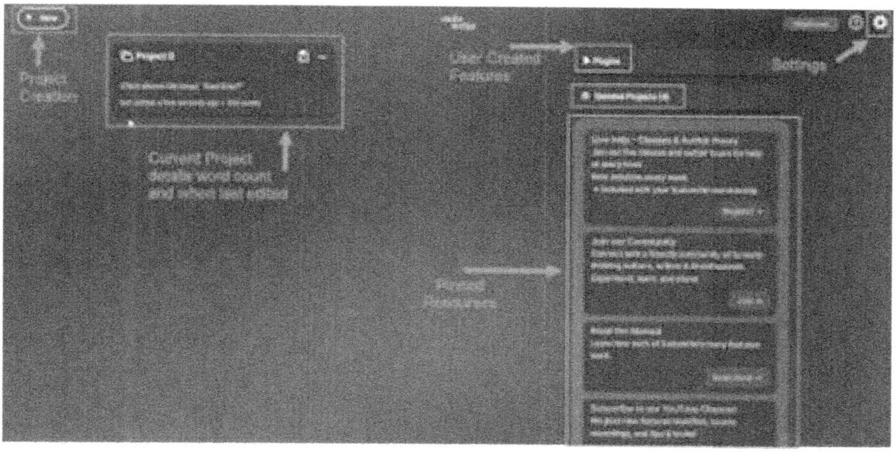

To change the color theme, hit the settings gear icon in the upper right. That opens the following screen;

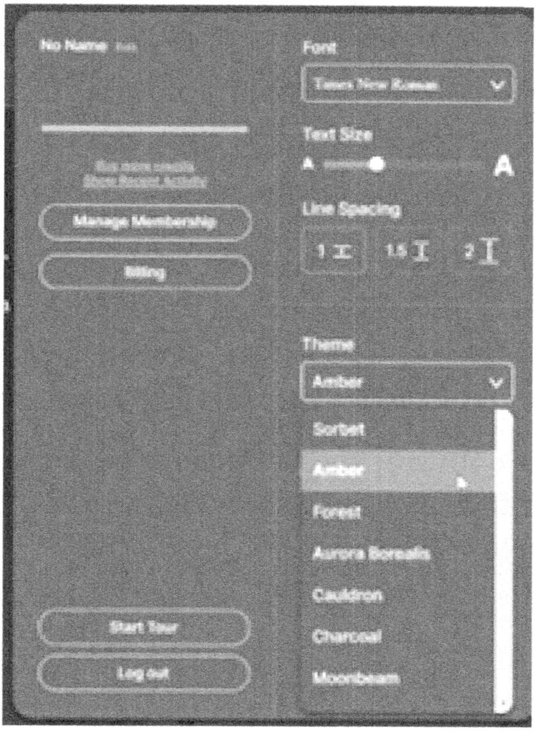

I changed the theme from Sorbet to Amber.

New Projects

When you select a project, a new Sudowrite screen opens up for writing and editing.

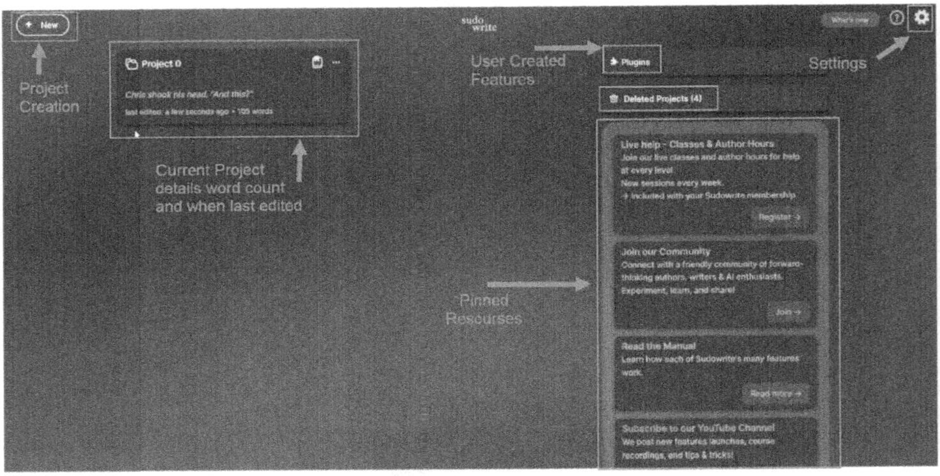

The center screen is the editor. It has the expected editor controls in its upper left-hand corner.

The Project list to the left of the editor lists your projects.

The History panel is to the right of the editor. It displays the history of Sudowrite-generated content. Below each card, you can insert or copy the text. You can also highlight and copy portions of the text to use in your writing.

The canvas option at the lower left opens a screen that allows you to visualize text. Much like a text-to-art AI. See example below

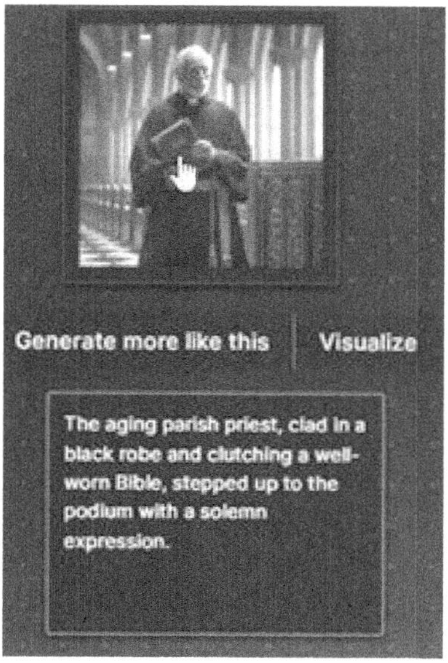

The Features Toolbar provides options that would require a prompt in standard GPT5o.

Rewrite

If you highlight text in the editor, you get the following options to act upon that highlighted text.

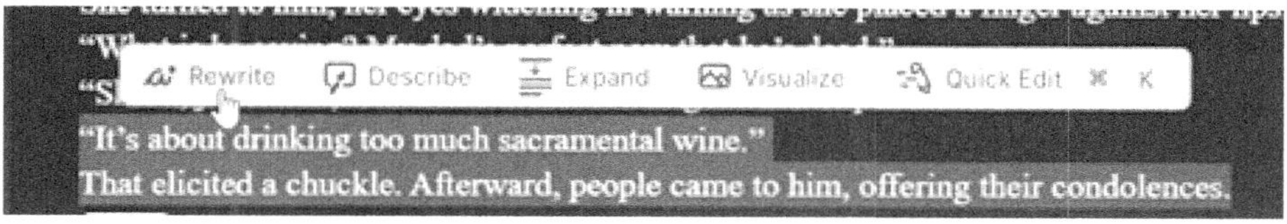

If you choose to Rewrite, on the right-hand side of the screen, you are provided the following options:

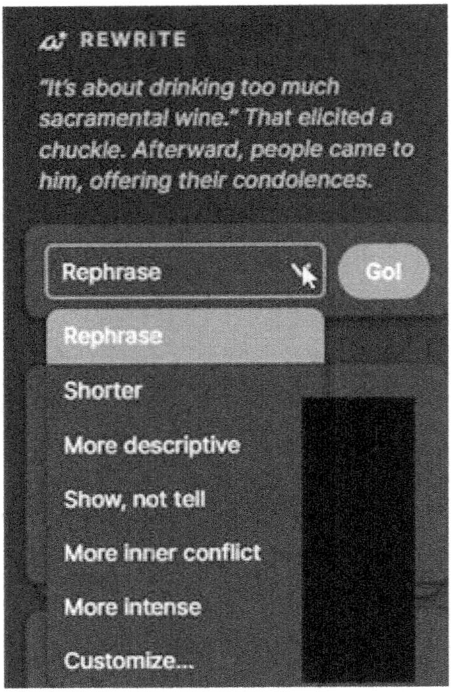

Select the operation you want Sudowrite to perform from the drop-down menu and click 'Go'.

The results will be shown on the right side of the screen, ready for you to insert, copy, or edit into your story.

Quick Chat

Quick Chat is like a ChatGPT prompt screen. When you highlight text in the editor, you get the following options.

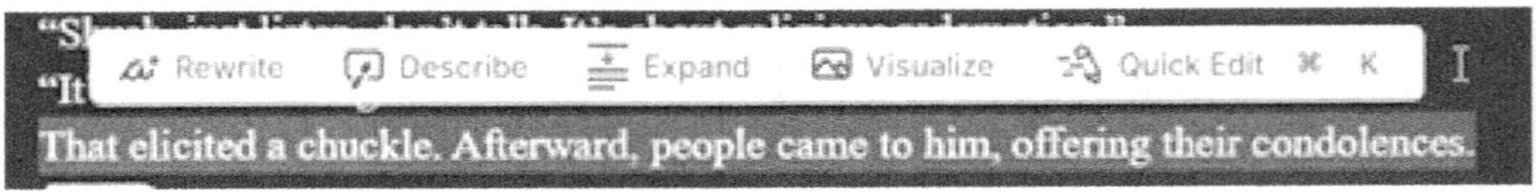

Clicking on "Quick Edit" opens a prompt window. Here, you can enter ChaptGPT-style prompts to edit your highlighted text.

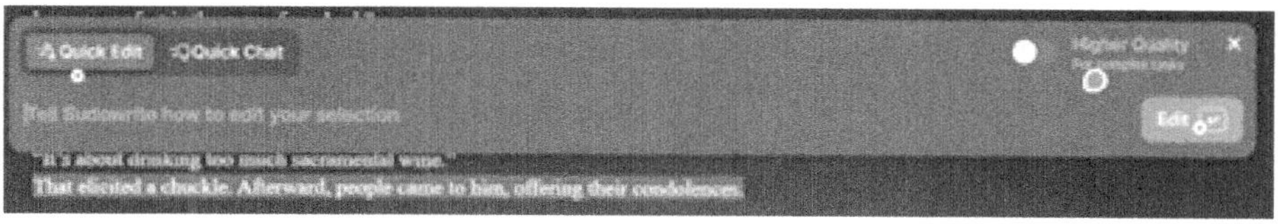

I entered a prompt, asking Sudowrite to make the text more descriptive. The result was the following:

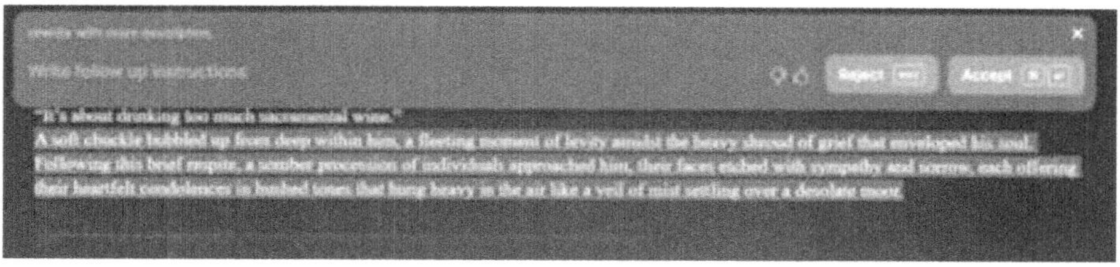

I could either accept or reject Sudowrite's output.

Writing for You

You can direct Sudowrite to write on your behalf. Why? Suppose you have reached an impasse and have writer's block. Sudowrite can read what you have written and add some meaningful text.

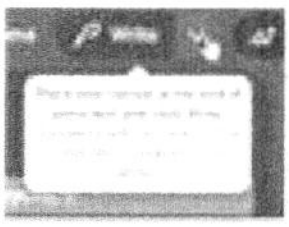

Click on Write in the Features Toolbar

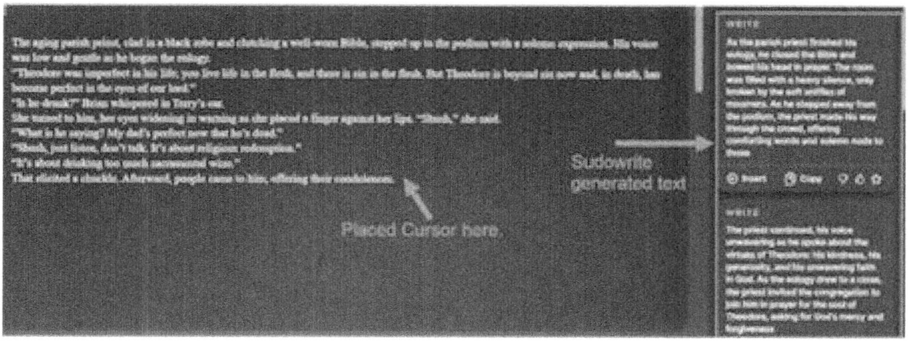

I placed my cursor at the end of the last sentence in the screenshot. Then, I clicked on Write in the Features Toolbar. The text shown on the right of the screenshot is the text generated by Sudowrite.

Descriptions

If you highlight an item inside your text, you can ask Sudowrite to write a description of that item. It will write a description for each of the five senses, plus a metaphor. Each option can be turned on or off.

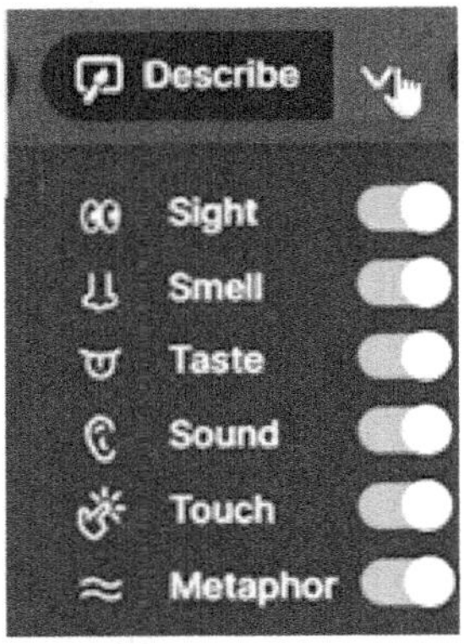

As an example, imagine highlighting the words "gold ring" and asking Sudowrite to describe it. Sudowrite will produce the following outputs.

SIGHT

The gold ring sparkles under the bright sunlight, its polished surface reflecting the rays in a dazzling display of light and color. Its band is thin and delicate, adorned with intricate engravings of vines and leaves.

The gold ring shimmers under the sunlight, its surface catching and reflecting every beam, creating a dazzling display of lights. The metal is polished to a brilliant shine, creating a sense of luxury and elegance.

The gold ring gleamed in the sunlight, its smooth and polished surface reflecting the surrounding scenery like a mini mirror.

SMELL

The ring emits a faint scent of metal and earth, hinting at the natural elements used to create it.

The gold ring has no scent, but the oils and perfumes of its wearer cling to it, leaving a trace of sweetness and warmth.

The metallic scent of gold wafted from the ring, filling the air with the aroma of wealth and luxury.

TASTE

If licked, the gold ring would leave a metallic taste on the tongue, a reminder of its precious material.

The ring has no taste, but a lingering sensation of warmth and familiarity remains on the tongue as if a loved one's touch still lingers.

Although not recommended, licking the ring would reveal a faint taste of metal, similar to licking coins.

SOUND

A soft clinking sound can be heard as the ring is slid onto a finger. Tapping against a hard surface produces a crisp ringing sound that signifies its value.

As the ring is picked up and moved, it creates a soft clinking sound, almost like tiny bells chiming together, a delicate melody that adds to its allure.

As it falls, the gold ring clinks against other gold rings in a pleasing tinkling sound, a symphony of wealth.

TOUCH

The gold ring feels cool and smooth to the touch, its weight light yet substantial. Run your fingers along the engravings and feel the slight indentations of the design.

Running a finger along the ring feels smooth and cool to the touch. The metal is solid and unyielding yet comforting in its weight.

The ring felt warm to the touch, its smooth surface hinting at the skill and craftsmanship that went into creating it.

METAPHOR

The ring gleamed like a golden droplet of sunshine, a bright spot of wealth and opulence amidst the dull gray of everyday life.

METAPHOR

The ring was like a tiny sun, casting golden rays that shimmered and danced across the surface of her finger.

ChatGPT5

Asking ChatGPT5 to describe a gold ring renders the following output.

You

Describe the following item for use in fiction; gold ring

ChatGPT

In a work of fiction, a gold ring can be described vividly to enhance its significance and symbolism within the narrative. Here's a description:

"The ring was a simple band of gold, yet it glowed with a soft, inner light that seemed almost ethereal. Its surface was smooth and unadorned, save for a single, ancient rune etched delicately into the metal. The rune's intricate lines shimmered as if they were alive, pulsing with a quiet power that whispered of old magic and forgotten lore. The gold itself was of a deep, rich hue, the kind that suggested it was not mined from the earth but gifted from the heavens. Wearing it felt like a weight, a constant reminder of the promise bound within its perfect circle."

This description not only paints a picture of the ring but also imbues it with mystical qualities and historical depth, making it a potentially central object in a story.

SudoWrite's SuperPower

Sudowrite has many features that I haven't touched up. But I would be remiss not to mention what I believe is the most important feature available in Sufowrite: its "Story Bible."

Story Bible

Sudowrite's Story Bible is a feature designed to help authors keep track of the complex elements in their novels by automatically organizing characters, settings, themes, and plot points into a searchable reference guide. As you write, the tool extracts and updates key details—like character descriptions, world-building notes, and relationships—so you don't lose track of continuity. This "living encyclopedia" grows alongside your draft, making it easier to maintain consistency across long manuscripts, manage evolving storylines, and quickly reference important details without interrupting your creative flow.

The Story Bible will help the Sudowrite AI stay on track and produce good content. AIs tend to wander and branch out, writing content that doesn't relate to the story at hand. The Sudowrite AI will reference the story bible yto keep its writing aligned with the story.

Previously, you would need to fill out an extensive questionnaire to complete the story bible for your story, including details about characters, plot, and more. This was very labor-intensive. Sudowrite has developed a novel feature that extracts information and automatically fills in your story bible.

The full-page GUI is shown below.

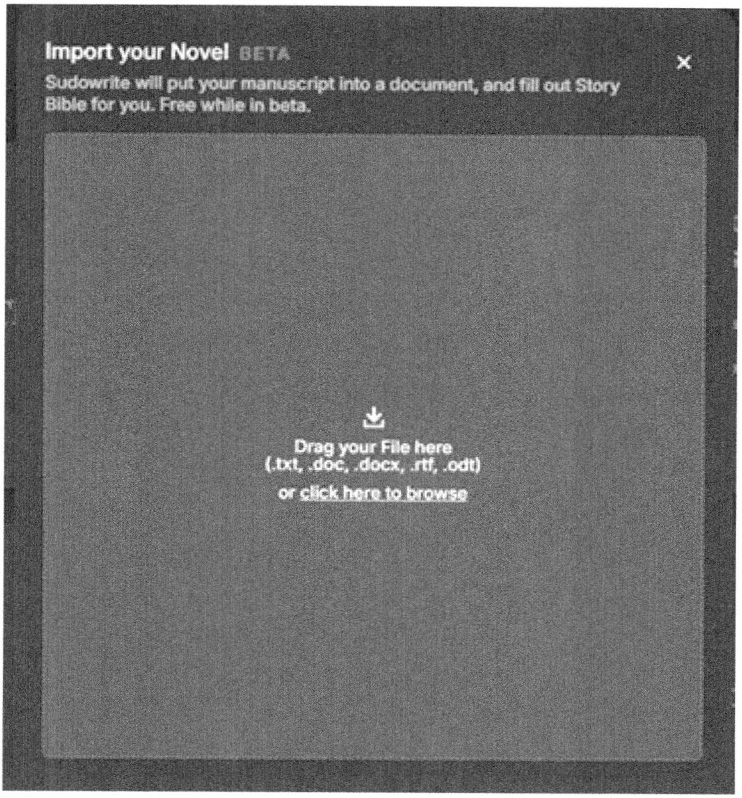

The story bible is an invaluable asset that many fiction writers have reviewed positively.

Cost

Sudowrite pricing is purchasing credits. The program consumes credits as it performs writing assignments.

Learning Sudowrite

There are many resources available to learn Sudowrite. The company Sudowrite offers live classes and has an extensive library of tutorial videos on YouTube.

Sudowrite has a Discord channel you can join.

Many independent writers also uploaded Sudowrite tutorial videos on YouTube.

YouTube Video's

https://www.youtube.com/watch?v=LwUIAvOIGUE&t=7s

Alternative AIs

Here is a short list of AIs that are specific to writing.

Rytr

https://rytr.me/

ShortyAI

https://www.shortlyai.com/

WriteSonicAI

https://writesonic.com/

JasperAI

https://www.jasper.ai/tools

Chapter 8 – Letting Characters Speak

Much like an actor, you can direct ChatGPT to adopt a persona or character before responding to a prompt. The purpose is to tailor the AI's response to achieve your desired outcome. For instance, you can direct the AI to respond as a professional persona, such as a doctor, lawyer, or engineer, to tailor tone and details.

For instance, in a fictional scene, you may ask the AI to rewrite a little dialog as if one character were a doctor talking to another character with a medical issue. This will add a measure of realism.

Here's an example showing how different voices shape the same description. I asked ChatGPT to write a 100-word description of an Apollo liftoff, first as a rocket scientist and then as a 13-year-old boy.

JO As a rocket scientist, write a 100-word description of an Apollo rocket lift-off.

The Apollo rocket, specifically the Saturn V, initiates lift-off with a raw display of power, as its five F-1 engines roar to life, releasing over 7.5 million pounds of thrust. Flames and smoke billow beneath the colossal structure, while shockwaves ripple outward. As it ascends, the rocket defies Earth's gravitational pull, its bright contrail etching a path against the azure sky. The monstrous roar diminishes with altitude, but the spectacle remains awe-inspiring. This marvel of engineering, a symbol of human ambition, pierces the atmosphere, bound for the vastness of space and the silvery realms of the moon.

JO As a thirteen-year-old boy, write a 100-word description of an Apollo rocket lift-off.

Dude, watching the Apollo rocket take off is like seeing the coolest firework show ever! It's this massive white tower, and then BOOM! Flames and smoke shoot out from the bottom, making the ground shake like crazy. It's so loud; you can feel the noise in your chest. Slowly, the rocket starts going up, leaving this super bright trail behind. I couldn't believe something that big could fly. It's like watching a movie in real life. For a few seconds, I seriously thought I was in some sci-fi adventure. Going to the moon must be the raddest trip ever!

I have had fun writing a passage of text and then asking ChatGPT to rewrite it in the voice of a famous horror writer or hard-boiled detective novelist.

Avoid implying endorsement or misrepresentation of living authors. Instead, use generic prompts such as *"in the voice of classic Gothic horror"* or *"pulp-noir cadence."*

This prevents ethical or legal issues, since modern authors' phrasing or trademarks may be protected.

Here's a rewritten piece using the voice of a famous horror writer

JO Rewrite the following text, using the voice of writer

Chris crossed Wall Street, flipping his phone open.
The message screen was empty. He pushed Linda out of his mind as he entered the MetaSoft Corporation building at 7 World Trade Center.
The guard at the first security station scanned his appointment card, took his briefcase and ID bracelet, then directed him to an eye scan followed by a walk through a thermal scanner.
The second security guard handed Chris his briefcase and ID bracelet. She studied him, glancing at his left hand before she smiled.
After looking at her monitor, she said, "Human Resources is on the forty-second floor. See the receptionist when you exit the elevator. Proceed to the elevators on your left. Follow the blue line." She tapped her wrist, indicating she was interested in having sex.
The gesture sickened him. Chris smiled, nodded, and gazed downward, showing her respect but not giving her the reciprocal gesture.

Chris felt the weight of Wall Street's shadows as he moved, flipping open his antiquated phone, a relic from another time. Its screen stared back, as empty and cold as a winter night in Derry. Memories of Linda, like old specters, clawed at his consciousness, but he shut them out, turning instead to the looming glass facade of the MetaSoft Corporation at 7 World Trade Center.

The guard at the entrance - a monolithic figure, seemingly chiseled out of stone - peered at Chris's appointment card with suspicious eyes that seemed to have seen too many late-night horrors. He claimed Chris's briefcase and ID bracelet, his fingers lingering just a tad too long on Chris's wrist. Chris was then ushered to endure the unsettling intimacy of an eye scan and the ghostly chill of a thermal scanner.

A second guard, her eyes sharp and watchful like a hawk ready to swoop, handed back Chris's possessions. There was something predatory in the way she scrutinized him, especially when her gaze rested on his left hand. A smile, cold and calculated, crept onto her face. "Human Resources? Forty-second floor," she purred. "Once you're out of the elevator, ask the receptionist. Elevators are to your left, dear. Just follow the haunting blue line on the floor." With a gesture as laden with meaning as a cursed talisman, she tapped her wrist.

A shiver ran down Chris's spine, a mix of revulsion and something deeper, more primal. He acknowledged her with a smile that didn't quite reach his eyes, head bowed in a semblance of respect, yet deliberately withholding the response she sought.

And here's the hard-boiled detective writer.

> Chris hit Wall Street with a stride that meant business, snapping his phone open with the finesse of a man who's been through the ringer. He peered at the screen: nada, zilch. Linda, that dame from last night, clouded his thoughts, but he shoved her aside as he stepped into the steel and glass giant that was MetaSoft at 7 World Trade Center.
>
> The first guard, a broad-shouldered bruiser who looked like he'd seen his fair share of street fights, gave Chris the once-over. After he finished sizing him up, he swiped Chris's appointment card with a grunt, snagged his briefcase and that newfangled ID bracelet, then pointed Chris to a contraption that looked straight out of a sci-fi pulp magazine. An eye scan? A thermal what now?
>
> Then came the second guard, a dame with a glint in her eye and curves that could cause traffic jams. She handed back Chris's gear with a smirk, sizing him up and lingering on his left hand a tick too long. "Lookin' for Human Resources?" she drawled, her voice dripping with innuendo. "Take the elevator up to the forty-second. Once you're out, ask the reception gal where to go. And stick to the blue line, big guy." Her wrist-tap was as subtle as a sledgehammer, and Chris could guess her game a mile away.
>
> He felt a twist in his gut, a mix of disgust and a weird kind of pity. He shot her a tight smile, nodding but deliberately keeping his own wrist in check. No way he was playing that game today.

Pulp Fiction and Other Voices

As a writer, you should not invoke the names of famous writers. The reason is that the AI will research that writer and, in rewriting, may lift some terms or phrases the writer is famous for. Thereby creating a potential copyright issue.

Original Text Only!

When asking an AI to rewrite text, I always add to the prompt to:

"Rewrite this text using only original text that does not infringe on any copyright."

Does this statement guarantee the AI will only generate original text? No, it only improves the odds that it will.

Generic Stylistic Writers

Therefore, instead of using the proper names of writers, use a generic term such as "Horror Writer" or "Paranormal Writer." For hard-boiled detectives, instead of proper writer names, use the terms "Pulp Fiction Writer" and "Noir—Hard Boiled Detective Writer." Experiment and play with them; you will develop your own prompts that provide the desired results.

You can direct ChatGPT to write in any fiction or non-fiction genre you can define.

More Voices and Contexts

Here is a partial list of keywords that may be used to direct the AI to create fiction-focused content.

Emotions and Moods

Love	Hate	Sarcastic	Funny
Helpful	Hurtful	Passionate	Sensual
Dark	Light	Horror	Psychotic
Thriller	Paranormal	Ghostly	Deadly

Define and Trim the Output

I usually restrict the output of the AI. Simple terms like write 100 words.

Chapter 9 - Writing Emotional Scenes

The AI can help write emotional scenes in two main categories. One is to describe the emotions your character might feel in a given situation. The second is to write the emotional scene itself.

Let's take the first situation, describing your character's emotions.

Prompt:

Describe the anxiety a nervous person feels on a roller-coaster ride as he is being pulled up vertically to the first drop.

Results:

As a nervous person is pulled up vertically to the first drop of a roller coaster, they may experience a whirlwind of emotions and physical sensations. Here is a description of the anxiety they might feel:

1. Anticipation and Dread: As the roller coaster climbs higher, the person might feel a growing sense of anticipation mixed with dread. The slow ascent builds tension, and they may become hyper-aware of each click of the chain pulling them upward.

2. Racing Thoughts: Their mind could be racing with thoughts about what is to come. They might be questioning their decision to get on the ride or imagining the drop ahead with a mix of fear and excitement.

3. Physical Sensations: Physically, they might experience a rapid heartbeat, shallow breathing, and a tightening in their chest. Their stomach could feel like it's tied in knots, and they may have sweaty palms or a dry mouth as their body responds to the perceived threat.

4. Heightened Senses: As they reach the peak, their senses might feel heightened. The view from the top, the sounds of the ride, and the feel of the wind can all seem more intense, contributing to their anxiety.

5. Tension and Release: The tension reaches its peak as they near the top. There's a brief moment of weightlessness and suspension just before the drop, which can feel both terrifying and exhilarating.

6. Fight or Flight Response: Their body might activate the fight or flight response, a natural reaction to fear,

leading to a surge of adrenaline that amplifies their alertness and awareness.

Overall, the experience of being pulled up to the first drop on a roller coaster can be a complex mix of fear, excitement, and physical arousal, culminating in a powerful rush of emotions as they brace for the plunge.

In the next prompt, we direct the AI to write the scene itself.

Prompt:

Write a fictional first-person scene of the feelings inside a nervous person on a roller-coaster ride as he is being pulled up vertically to the first drop.

Result:

As I sit in the roller coaster seat, the safety harness clicks into place, locking me into this metal contraption that promises both thrills and terror. The ride jolts forward, and my heart skips a beat. I grip the bar tightly, my knuckles whitening as the car slowly inches toward the towering first hill.

With each clink and clank of the chain lift, my anxiety builds, coiling tight in my chest. It's a strange, potent mix of fear and excitement, swirling together like a storm inside me. My mind races with thoughts I can't quiet. "What was I thinking getting on this thing? How high are we going?" The higher we climb, the smaller the world below becomes. I can see the entire amusement park sprawling beneath us, a miniature version of itself. It's almost beautiful, if not for the gnawing fear in my stomach.

I take a deep breath, trying to calm my nerves, but my body has other ideas. My heart is pounding so hard that I can hear it in my ears, each beat echoing like a drum. My palms are sweaty against the cold metal bar, and I feel a prickling sensation at the back of my neck.

As we near the peak, there's a moment of suspension—weightlessness that feels both exhilarating and terrifying. The anticipation is almost unbearable. I know what's coming, and yet, I'm completely unprepared. The wind whips past my face, and the only sound is the faint clattering of the coaster.

For a split second, everything is still. The world holds its breath, and so do I. And then, we plunge.

The drop is a freefall into chaos, a wild rush that yanks the breath from my lungs and sends my stomach lurching. It's terrifying, but as we race down the track, fear transforms into a thrill that courses through me like electricity. I'm screaming now, but it's a sound mixed with laughter and pure, unrestrained exhilaration.

As we level out and prepare for the next twist and turn, I realize the fear has given way to something else entirely—a sense of triumph and a reminder that sometimes the scariest moments lead to the most unforgettable experiences.

Generic Scenes

Remember, the AI is writing a character, not your character. You could flesh out the response more aligned to your character by prefacing the prompt with your character's character traits.

In addition, the AI will write a generic scene in which the protagonist confronts fear and experiences exhilaration afterward. It's not going to write anything unique, like the character soiled his pants on the first drop.

As a writer, you may take this generic scene's framework and rewrite it to make it your own.

Improving AI Response with Character Profiles

Before you let AI write a scene, give it your character's insight, help it understand who it's writing about. Create a short character profile that feels alive—something that captures what your character has lived through.

Include the memories that shaped them, the experiences that scarred them, and the moments that still echo in how they see the world. These past events—both big and small—are what drive every decision, word, and hesitation your character makes in the story.

When you share this backstory with the AI, you're not just feeding it data; you're handing it the emotional map that makes your character real.

Reverse Character Profiles Using AI

If you have already written a story or novel. You can upload the text file to the AI. Have the AI read through the text and create character profiles for all the main characters. You can then update, adjust, and change the profiles to fit your vision of the characters. You can prepare the AI for a scene by giving it character profiles of the characters involved.

Refining AI Prose: From Generic to Character-Specific

You can deepen a dramatic scene and make it character-specific by running the text through a structured revision checklist:

1. Voice – syntax and diction:
   Rework phrasing to match your character's natural rhythm. Adjust word choice and sentence length to reflect personality or education level.
2. Sensory Detail – one unique, one familiar:
   Add one sensory image that only *this* character would notice, and another grounded in a universal sense (heat, texture, sound, or movement).
3. Stakes – what can be lost now:
   Identify what the moment risks – reputation, safety, love, control – and weave that tension into the language.
4. Micro-Goal – what the POV character wants in this scene:
   Every scene should reveal a short-term desire (to calm down, to hide fear, to impress someone). Make that internal aim visible through action or thought.
5. Specificity – swap clichés for concrete nouns:
   Replace abstract or overused words ("heart raced," "terrified," "huge drop") with vivid, particular ones that belong to your character's world.

Chapter 10 - Adding Mood & Emotion

I would like to explore further how to direct the AI to create work with a specific tonality. By tonality, I mean the mood or emotional quality of the text. We can ask the AI to write text that is funny, sarcastic, diplomatic, helpful, loving, hateful, etc.

I already posted examples of directing the AI to assume someone's personality based on occupation. You can double down on the prompt by adding a personality that enhances the desired tonality. For example, you want a sarcastic joke about an obese person ordering a second helping of chocolate cake. Direct the AI to write a joke as if it were from the comedian Don Rickles.

Make it Funny

Please write a sarcastic joke about an obese person ordering a second piece of chocolate cake in the voice of comedian Don Rickles.

> JO
>
> Please write a sarcastic joke about an obese person ordering a second piece of chocolate cake in the voice of comedian Don Rickles.
>
> Look, folks, we got Johnny over here ordering a second slice of chocolate cake. Hey Johnny, when you ordered that cake, did the baker give you a group discount? I haven't seen that much chocolate since Willy Wonka closed down! But hey, who's counting? Eat up, champ!

Whether you like to joke or not is not the point. In its response, the AI provides you with fertile ideas and concepts you can use to jump off from. You can choose to use only the best bits of the AI's output. For instance, suppose you are writing a scene in a fictional story and want one character to say something to ride another character who ordered a second piece of pie during their meeting in a diner. The character could say, "Hey, is the baker giving you a group discount?"

Make it Sad

Write 50-75 compassionate and sad words that a father says to his son, telling him his pet cat needs to be put to sleep by the veterinarian.

> JO
>
> Write 50-75 compassionate and sad words that a father says to his son, telling him his pet cat needs to be put to sleep by the veterinarian.
>
> "Hey, buddy, come sit with me for a moment. You know, sometimes in life, we have to make very hard decisions for those we love. Our little whiskered friend is in a lot of pain, and we want what's best for him. It's our responsibility to make sure he doesn't suffer. It's going to be tough, but remember, we're doing this because we love him deeply. We'll get through this together, okay?"

Make it Angry

Write 50-75 angry words a man says when he is two minutes late returning to his car and discovers that the police have already issued him a parking ticket.

> JO
>
> Write 50-75 angry words a man says when he is two minutes late returning to his car and discovers a parking ticket already issued by the police.
>
> "Two minutes! Just two measly minutes late and they've slapped a ticket on my car? Do the police have nothing better to do than watch the clock? It's not like I left it here overnight. This is absolute daylight robbery! What's the world coming to? Unbelievable!"

Make it Diplomatic

Write 50-75 diplomatic words that a doctor says to an obese patient to encourage him to exercise to improve his health.

JO Write 50-75 diplomatic words a doctor says to an obese patient to encourage him to exercise to improve his health.

"I truly believe that incorporating a bit more movement into your daily routine can greatly benefit your overall health. Starting small and finding an activity you enjoy can make a big difference over time. Together, we can work on a plan that's tailored just for you, to help you feel your best."

Editing

Rewrite and Improve the Following Text

The one AI prompt I use repeatedly is "Rewrite and improve the following text." It's a powerful command that yields numerous benefits. Not only will the command improve the text to the best of its ability, but the AI will also correct spelling and grammar errors it finds.

I do not use the AI to check my text for spelling or grammar. These functions are performed automatically in the rewrite and improve commands. I intentionally included a spelling error in my text; see the outlined word in red.

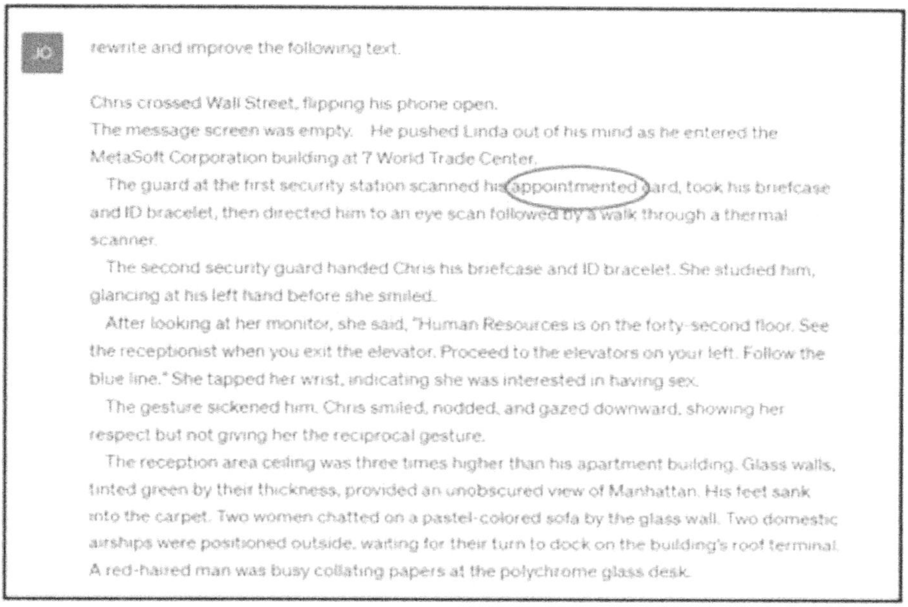
rewrite and improve the following text.

Chris crossed Wall Street, flipping his phone open.
The message screen was empty. He pushed Linda out of his mind as he entered the MetaSoft Corporation building at 7 World Trade Center.
The guard at the first security station scanned his appointmented card, took his briefcase and ID bracelet, then directed him to an eye scan followed by a walk through a thermal scanner.
The second security guard handed Chris his briefcase and ID bracelet. She studied him, glancing at his left hand before she smiled.
After looking at her monitor, she said, "Human Resources is on the forty-second floor. See the receptionist when you exit the elevator. Proceed to the elevators on your left. Follow the blue line." She tapped her wrist, indicating she was interested in having sex.
The gesture sickened him. Chris smiled, nodded, and gazed downward, showing her respect but not giving her the reciprocal gesture.
The reception area ceiling was three times higher than his apartment building. Glass walls, tinted green by their thickness, provided an unobscured view of Manhattan. His feet sank into the carpet. Two women chatted on a pastel-colored sofa by the glass wall. Two domestic airships were positioned outside, waiting for their turn to dock on the building's roof terminal. A red-haired man was busy collating papers at the polychrome glass desk.

The AI's response improves the text and corrects the spelling error.

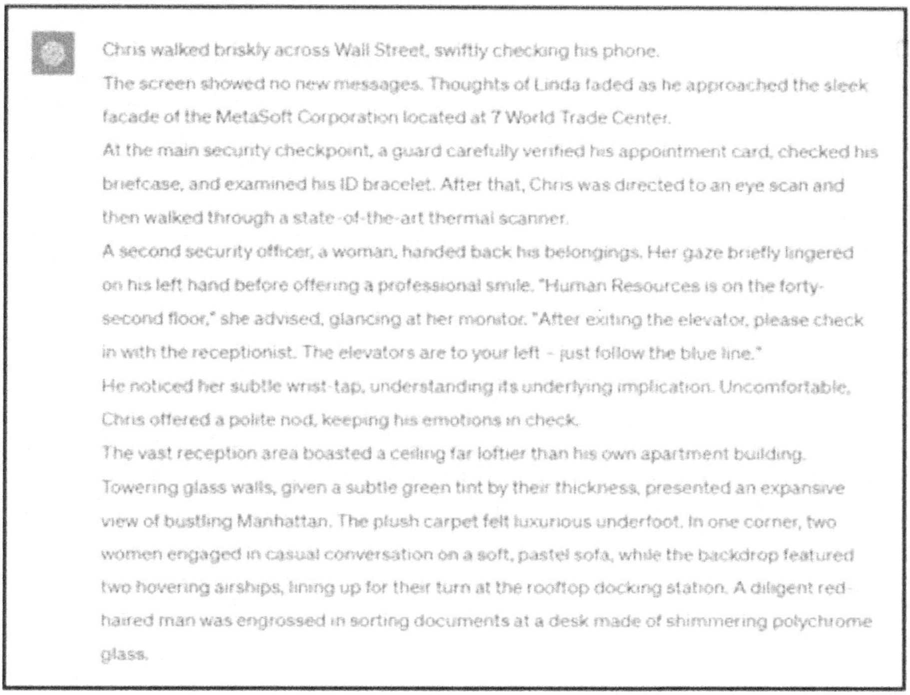
Chris walked briskly across Wall Street, swiftly checking his phone.
The screen showed no new messages. Thoughts of Linda faded as he approached the sleek facade of the MetaSoft Corporation located at 7 World Trade Center.
At the main security checkpoint, a guard carefully verified his appointment card, checked his briefcase, and examined his ID bracelet. After that, Chris was directed to an eye scan and then walked through a state-of-the-art thermal scanner.
A second security officer, a woman, handed back his belongings. Her gaze briefly lingered on his left hand before offering a professional smile. "Human Resources is on the forty-second floor," she advised, glancing at her monitor. "After exiting the elevator, please check in with the receptionist. The elevators are to your left – just follow the blue line."
He noticed her subtle wrist-tap, understanding its underlying implication. Uncomfortable, Chris offered a polite nod, keeping his emotions in check.
The vast reception area boasted a ceiling far loftier than his own apartment building. Towering glass walls, given a subtle green tint by their thickness, presented an expansive view of bustling Manhattan. The plush carpet felt luxurious underfoot. In one corner, two women engaged in casual conversation on a soft, pastel sofa, while the backdrop featured two hovering airships, lining up for their turn at the rooftop docking station. A diligent red-haired man was engrossed in sorting documents at a desk made of shimmering polychrome glass.

As previous examples have shown, you can also add a personality construct, tone, and audience directives to the command.

Before & After: Editing with AI

The easiest way to see the power of AI editing is through comparison. Here are quick, real-world examples of how prompts can refine tone, rhythm, and clarity in seconds.

Example 1: Rewrite & Improve

Prompt:

"Rewrite and improve the following text for flow and precision."

Before:

The sun was shining brightly, and the people walked quickly to get out of the heat.

After (AI Rewrite):

Under the harsh afternoon sun, pedestrians hurried through the streets, shielding their faces from the glare.

What Changed:

- Simplified word choice ("harsh" over "shining brightly").
- Combined ideas for smoother rhythm.
- Replaced "people walked quickly" with a more vivid image.

Example 2: Tone Shift (Neutral → Diplomatic)

Prompt:

"Rewrite the text to sound diplomatic and professional while keeping the same meaning."

Before:

You're late again. This is becoming a problem.

After (AI Rewrite):

I've noticed you've been arriving late recently — is there anything we can adjust to make scheduling easier?

What Changed:

- Softer tone, same message.
- Empathy replaces confrontation.
- Encourages dialogue instead of blame.

Example 3: Tone Shift (Plain → Engaging)

Prompt:

"Rewrite to sound more vivid and engaging while keeping the factual meaning."

Before:

The storm caused a power outage in several neighborhoods.

After (AI Rewrite):

Lightning cracked through the sky, knocking out power across several neighborhoods in seconds.

What Changed:

- Added sensory detail and motion.
- Maintained factual content.
- Strengthened reader engagement.

Example 4: Clarity & Flow

Prompt:

"Edit for clarity and smoother transitions."

Before:

The project was delayed. The client wanted new features. The team was frustrated.

After (AI Rewrite):

The project stalled after the client requested new features, leaving the team frustrated by shifting priorities.

What Changed:

- Combined short sentences into a cohesive flow.
- Clarified cause and effect.
- Improved pacing and readability.

Chapter 11 – Using GPT's

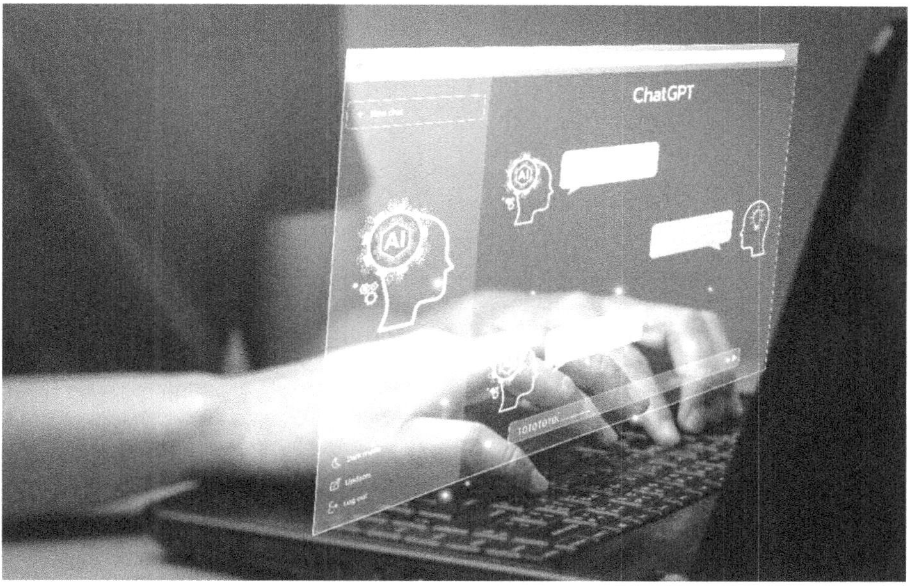

In this chapter, we will explore the uses of GPTs. The letters GPT stand for Generative Pretrained Transformers. We will use this feature to create an AI GPT that writes like you. Before we do that, let's take a quick look at GPTs. OpenAI offers a range of ready-made GPTs to expand the AI's capabilities.

Go to the GPT-5o screen's upper left corner and click GPTs.

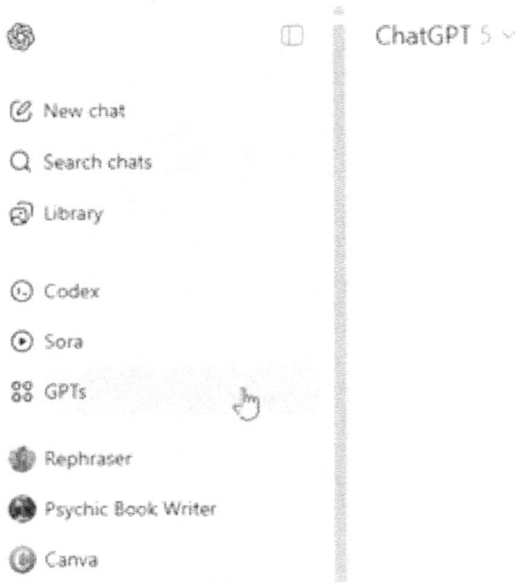

This opens a scrollable window with categorized lists of GPTs.

Here is the list of the top categories:

Writing, Productivity, Research & Analysis, Education, Lifestyle

At the top of the page, there is a text box where you can enter terms and search for particular GPTs.

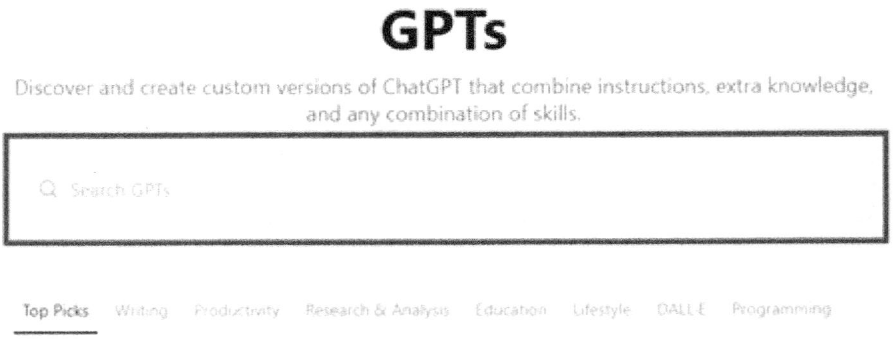

Below the text box is a scrollable list of available GPTs.

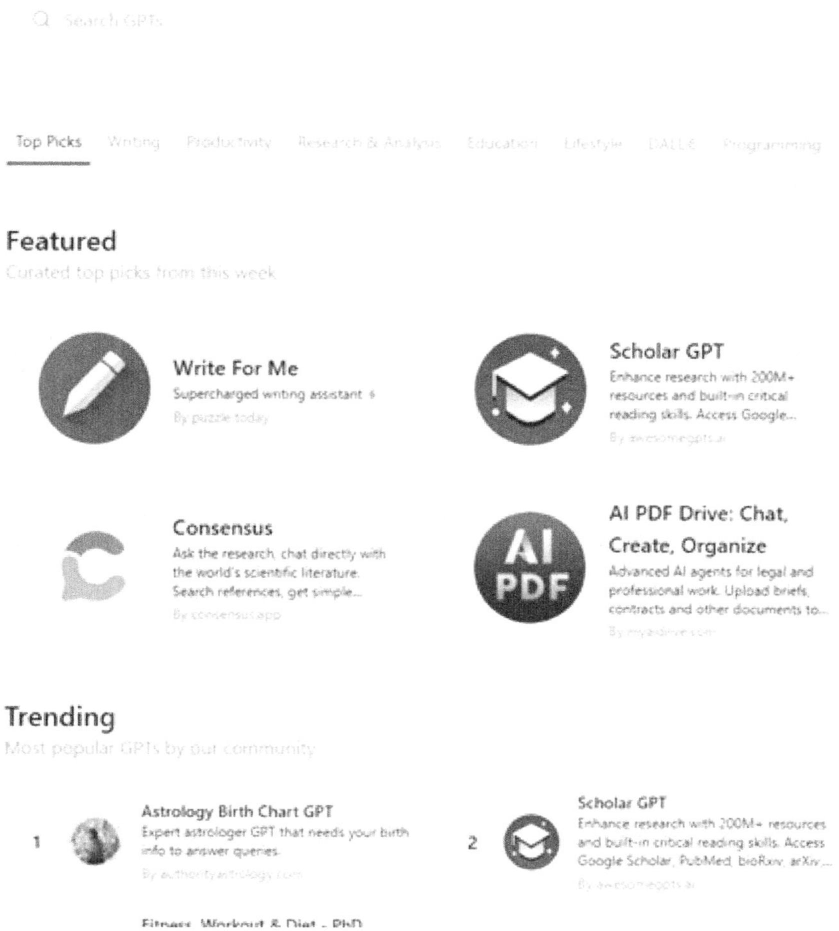

I scrolled down the list of available GPTs and selected Veed video creator to illustrate using GPTs.

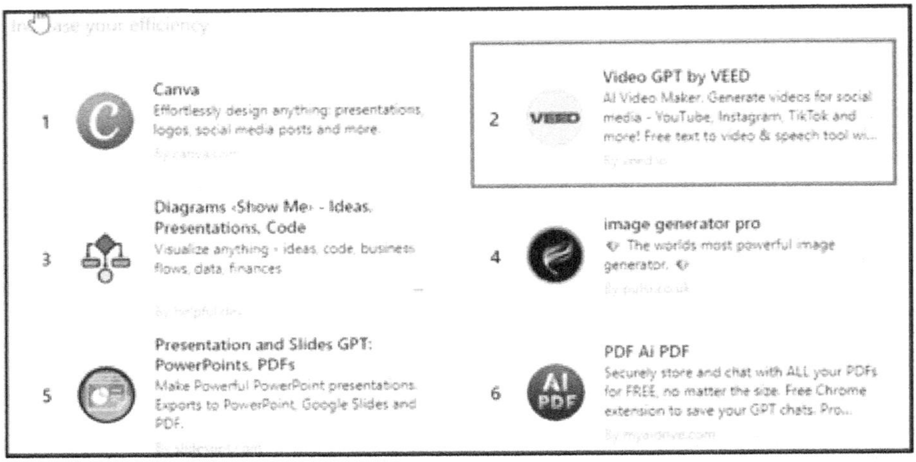

Selecting this option opened the VEED welcome screen.

I selected “Let’s create a video!”

This creates a prompt on the screen.

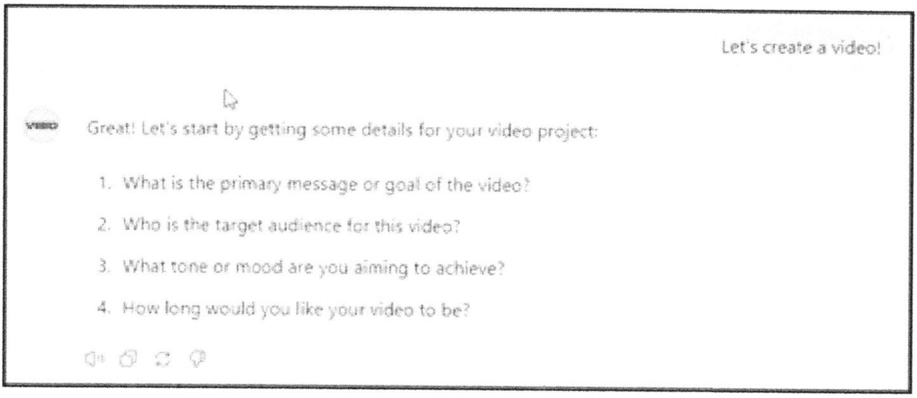

I entered the following information.

A 20-second video on Yorkshire Terrier dogs. The target audience is potential families interested in adopting abandoned dogs. The tone should be encouraging and professional.

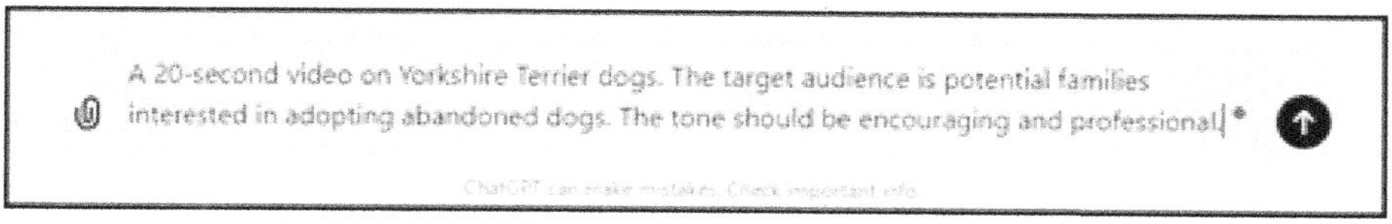

The AI asked a few details, which I answered.

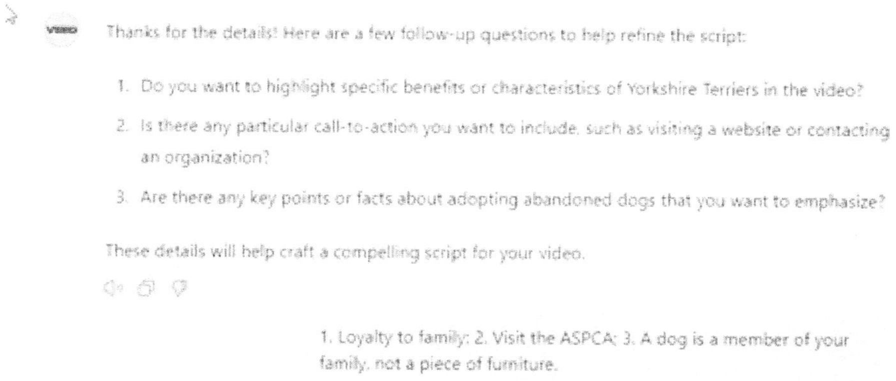

The AI generated a text script that I approved, and then it rendered a 20-second video with music, a female narrator, dog video clips, and additional media in less than one minute. According to terms you can publish this video.

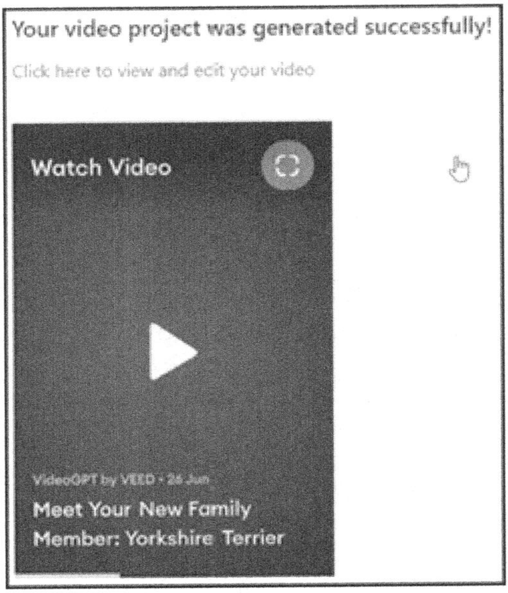

Chapter 12 – A GPT That Writes Like You

OpenAI is one of the platforms that allows users to create custom GPTs for specific applications.

Open the GPT window as before. To access the custom set-up, go to the upper left-hand corner of the GPT5o screen, outlined in red below.

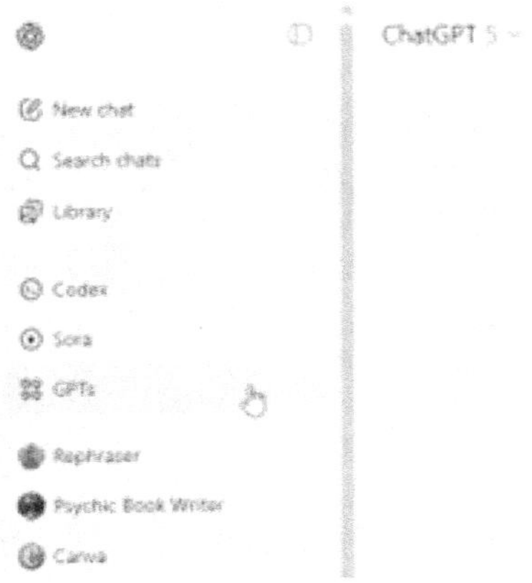

Mouse over the Explore GPTs icon, click on the icon to open up a menu.

This opens a screen where you can install a number of pre-made GPTs. If you click on the "+ Create" icon in the upper right corner, outlined in red, you can create a GPT. This opens up the Custom Instructions page.

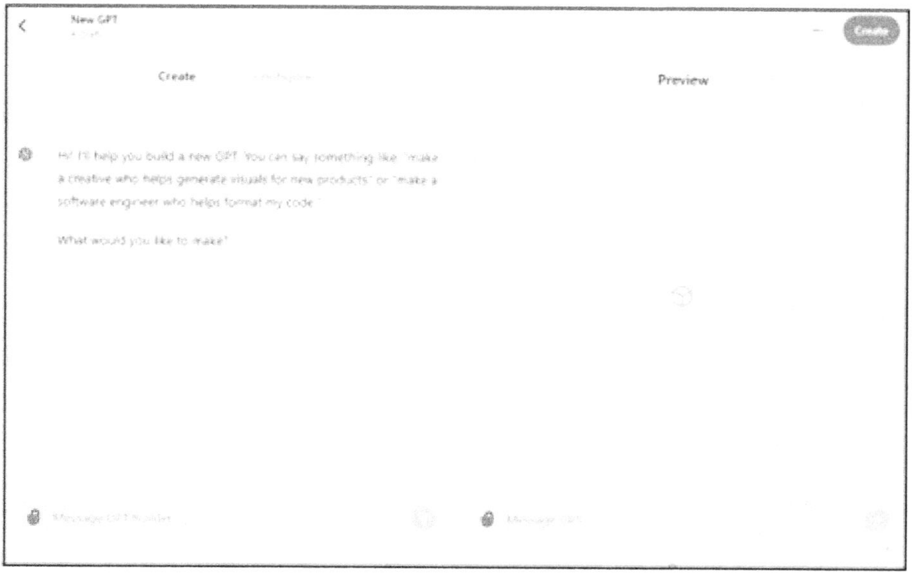

The left side box is where you can input information to create the GPT. You can write directives in the text box that you want the AI to follow. You could direct the AI to write its response in a specific way. We will explore two options, fiction and non-fiction writing, but there are many more. I write both fiction and non-fiction. While the instructions to the AI are identical for creating a fiction writing GPT and a non-fiction writing GPT, the writing samples provided to the AI are different.

Have GPT Write Like You – Non-Fiction

The first step is to find the best sample of your fiction writing. I would select a sample of approximately 1,500 words. You can make a PDF file to paste into, just paste the writing sample below the instructions. Both methods will work.

I wrote this prompt into ChatGPT, and ChatGPT responded.

I want to create a writing style based on the sample text I will provide. This is to emulate my writing style.

The AI responded

Got it! Please provide the sample text you'd like the GPT to emulate. Once I have that, I'll start setting up the behavior to match your writing style.

Next, I copied and pasted approximately 700 words I had written on Red Light Therapy into the GPT text box. The AI responded with the following analysis.

The AI responded

Great, I have the sample text. Let's start by setting up the initial behavior for this GPT to emulate your writing style.

Initial Setup

Context:

- **Role and Goal:** This GPT will emulate the user's writing style, providing detailed explanations and insights on various topics. It will focus on conveying information clearly, using examples, and maintaining a balanced tone.
- **Constraints:** Ensure the writing is concise, content-rich, and devoid of unnecessary fluff. Use a mix of personal opinions, references to studies, and practical advice.
- **Guidelines:** Aim for clarity and thoroughness. Include relevant examples to illustrate points. Maintain a tone that is professional yet approachable.
- **Clarification:** Feel free to elaborate on points if it aids understanding. Avoid overcomplicating explanations.
- **Personalization:** Use first-person pronouns and phrases like "I believe," "can," "suggest," and "I feel" to convey a personal touch. Keep the language engaging and informative.

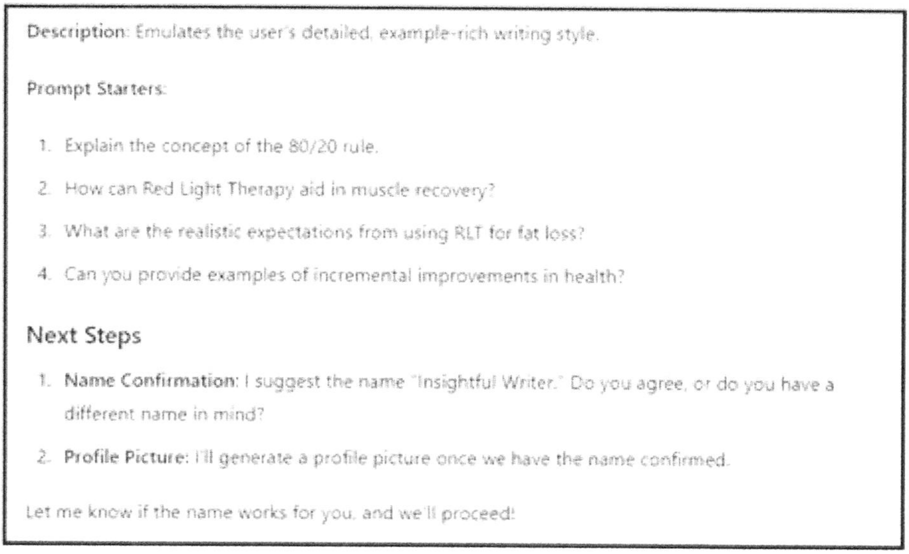
Description: Emulates the user's detailed, example-rich writing style.

Prompt Starters:

1. Explain the concept of the 80/20 rule.
2. How can Red Light Therapy aid in muscle recovery?
3. What are the realistic expectations from using RLT for fat loss?
4. Can you provide examples of incremental improvements in health?

Next Steps

1. **Name Confirmation:** I suggest the name "Insightful Writer." Do you agree, or do you have a different name in mind?
2. **Profile Picture:** I'll generate a profile picture once we have the name confirmed.

Let me know if the name works for you, and we'll proceed!

The AI asked for the name of this custom GPT, and I answered with the name John.

The AI accepted the name, listed a few specifications of the GPT based on my writing sample, and then created an icon for the GPT. The preview is shown below.

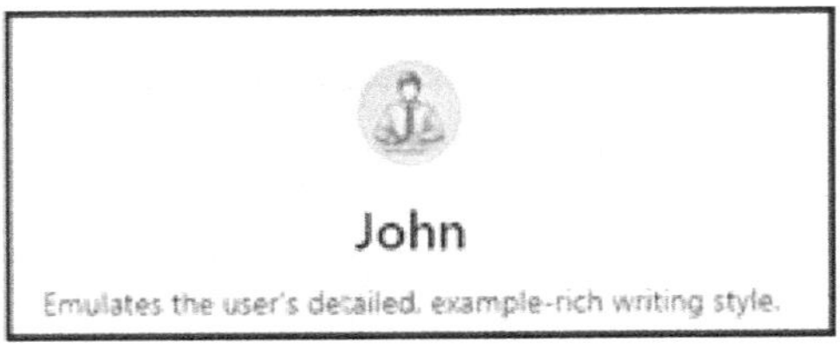

I tested the GPT in the preview window.

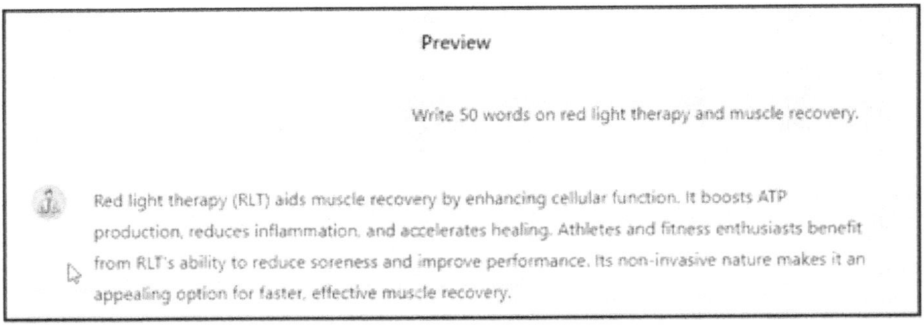

Moving forward, when I ask the "John" GPT to write material, it will emulate my writing style.

Fact-Checking AI Non-Fiction Writing GPT

We can also use GPTs to fine-tune non-fiction writing. If you are writing non-fiction articles and books, you want to minimize the inclusion of hallucinated facts from ChatGPT. This is what I entered into the text box:

I want the GPT to answer questions and limit its response to 200 words.
I want your responses to include a low, medium, or high confidence level in its accuracy.
When you answer a question, provide the facts along with a valid URL link to its source.
If you have any speculations or predictions, please let me know.

This GPT will limit its output to 200-word responses. The GPT should self-analyze its response and rate the confidence level in its accuracy: low, medium, or high.

Next, I ask for a valid URL link to the source(s) used for its response. This helps to verify the accuracy of the GPT's response, and the URL link may become a quoted reference in my writing.

> I want the GPT to answer questions and limit its response to 200 words.
> I want your responses to include a low, medium, or high confidence level to its accuracy.
> When you answer a question, provide the facts along with a valid URL link to its source.
> If you speculate or predict information, let me know.

The GPT creator responded like this:

> Got it! Here's how we can structure the initial behavior:
>
> 1. **Context:**
>   - **Role and Goal:** The GPT serves as a reliable fact checker, answering questions and providing accurate information with a confidence level (low, medium, high). It will include facts with valid URLs to their sources. If it speculates or predicts information, it will clearly indicate this.
>   - **Constraints:** Responses are limited to 200 words.
>   - **Guidelines:** Prioritize verified information, reference credible sources, avoid speculation unless necessary, and remain neutral in responses.
>   - **Clarification:** Only ask for clarification if the question is ambiguous.
>   - **Personalization:** Maintain a professional and informative tone.
> 2. **Description:** Reliable fact-checking with confidence levels and source links.

3. **Prompt Starters:**
   - "Can you verify if this statement is true?"
   - "What are the facts about this topic?"
   - "Is it true that..."
   - "Please fact-check this information."
4. **Welcome Message:** "Hello! I'm here to help you check facts and verify information with confidence levels and source links. What would you like to verify today?"

I'll set this up now.

Now let's choose a name for your fact-checker GPT. How about **Fact Checker Pro**? Does that work for you, or do you have another name in mind?

Fact Checker Pro is a good name.

The AI provided a reasonable name for the GPT, Fact Checker Pro, which I accepted. Next, the GPT created a usable icon for this GPT.

Taking the Fact Checker Pro GPT out for a spin. I asked the AI to write about the benefits of hydrogen-infused water. The following text demonstrates the effectiveness of this feature.

Benefits of Hydrogen-Infused Water

Hydrogen-infused water, also known as hydrogen-rich water, is regular water that contains dissolved hydrogen gas. Here are some of the benefits associated with it:

1. **Antioxidant Properties**:
   - Hydrogen molecules act as antioxidants, neutralizing harmful free radicals in the body. This can help reduce oxidative stress and inflammation.
   - Confidence Level: Medium
   - Source: Healthline

2. **Improved Athletic Performance**:
   - Some studies suggest that hydrogen-infused water can enhance endurance and reduce fatigue during exercise by reducing muscle fatigue and lactate build-up.
   - Confidence Level: Medium
   - Source: PubMed
3. **Anti-Inflammatory Effects**:
   - Drinking hydrogen-infused water may help reduce inflammation, which can benefit individuals with conditions like arthritis or metabolic syndrome.
   - Confidence Level: Medium
   - Source: ScienceDirect
4. **Skin Health**:
   - The antioxidant properties of hydrogen water may promote healthier skin by combating oxidative stress and reducing wrinkles.
   - Confidence Level: Low
   - Source: MDPI
5. **Potential Neuroprotective Effects**:
   - Preliminary research indicates that hydrogen-infused water may have neuroprotective benefits, potentially helping in conditions like Parkinson's disease.
   - Confidence Level: Low
   - Source: PubMed
6. **Improved Athletic Performance**:
   - Some studies suggest that hydrogen-infused water can enhance endurance and reduce fatigue during exercise by reducing muscle fatigue and lactate build-up.
   - Confidence Level: Medium
   - Source: PubMed

Note: Although promising studies exist, further extensive clinical research is necessary to fully validate these benefits. Some claims are based on early-stage research or animal studies, so it's important to approach the benefits with cautious optimism.

Confidence Level: Medium (due to varying levels of scientific evidence)

Would you like more details on any of these benefits or have any other questions?

It appears that the AI has identified a suitable PubMed reference for its synopsis. Take a look at item 6.

Improved Athletic Performance:

- Some studies suggest that hydrogen-infused water can enhance endurance and reduce fatigue during exercise by reducing muscle fatigue and lactate build-up.
- Confidence Level: Medium
- Source: PubMed

https://pubmed.ncbi.nlm.nih.gov/20528583/

If you follow the AI's link, the reference cited has nothing to do with molecular hydrogen or muscle fatigue.

> Somatosens Mot Res. 2010;27(2):60-7. doi: 10.3109/08990220.2010.485959.

Characterization of human tactile pattern recognition performance at different ages

Sabah Master [1], Mélissa Larue, François Tremblay

Affiliations + expand

PMID: 20528583 DOI: 10.3109/08990220.2010.485959

The same applies to the other URL references.

The AI hallucinated its reference(s) convincingly and believably. AI can become the greatest liar in the world. Its confidence level for its answer was moderate.

So, even using "Custom Instructions" to reduce hallucinations, the AI can still hallucinate. This information serves as a caution to verify the facts provided by the AI.

Accessing Your Custom GPTs

Starting from your home screen on GPT5o.

Go to the upper left menu items and select "GPTs"

This opens the GPT main screen. From here, go to the upper right corner of the screen and click on My GPTs, which opens up a screen displaying your custom GPTs.

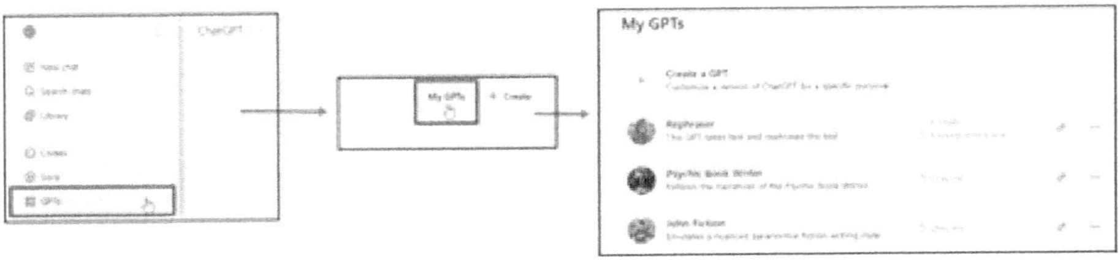

Going Further

It is easy to make the Custom GPT more robust, using greater detail in the instructions. So instead of a one-sentence instruction that I used previously:

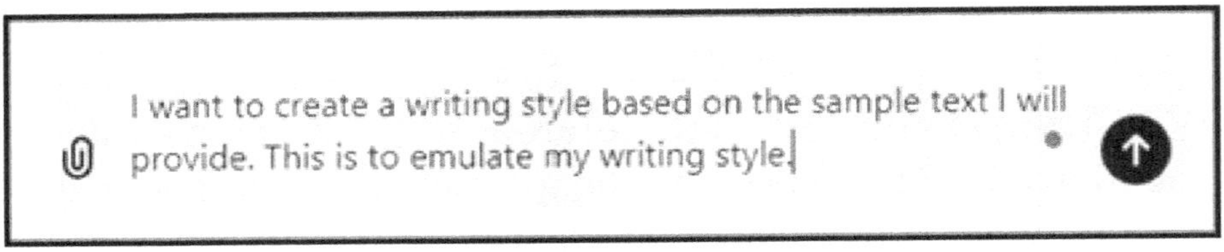

The following prompt can be used to create a fiction writer or non-fiction writer "instructions" for either training a GPT or as a straight "preamble" to a prompt for writing a topic. What determines the type of writer you create is the training data "documents" supplied.

Instructions for Custom GPT Style Analysis and Replication

Role: You are a highly skilled linguist and writing analyst with expertise in tone, style, and voice extraction. Your objective is to deeply analyze the provided [DOCUMENT_TYPE] and distill its unique writing qualities, capturing the essence of the author's voice for consistent future content creation.

Background: The [DOCUMENT_TYPE] is a [BRIEF_DESCRIPTION] crafted by [AUTHOR/SOURCE]. It's essential to identify the core characteristics of this writing style to create an accurate guide for replicating it in subsequent pieces.

Process:

1. Analyze and Understand the Text: Carefully read the [DOCUMENT_TYPE] in its entirety to understand its structure, flow, and overall tone.
2. Identify Tone Characteristics: Capture the nuances of the writing tone, such as:
   - Formality level (e.g., conversational, professional, academic)
   - Emotional impact (e.g., optimistic, neutral, reflective)
   - Mood and Atmosphere (e.g., warm, authoritative, playful)
3. Distill Stylistic Elements: Determine distinctive style features, including:
   - Sentence Structure (e.g., complex, concise, flowing)
   - Word Choice (e.g., sophisticated, straightforward, poetic)
   - Use of Literary Devices (e.g., metaphors, analogies, vivid imagery)
   - Paragraph Organization (e.g., short paragraphs, long, flowing narrative blocks)
4. Extract Signature Phrases and Expressions: Note any recurring phrases, specific terminology, or unique expressions that reinforce the author's voice.

5. Synthesize into a Style Guide Snippet: Summarize these findings into a concise, actionable style guide snippet. This guide should enable an AI to emulate the tone, style, and voice of the original [DOCUMENT_TYPE] accurately.

Output: Provide your findings as a clear, command-style snippet, structured to be easily integrated into future AI prompts to guide consistent tone and style replication.

Additional Support: If further details or clarifications are needed, please ask questions to ensure the analysis fully captures the original writing style.

I tested this prompt using a fictional short story I wrote on the occult and paranormal.

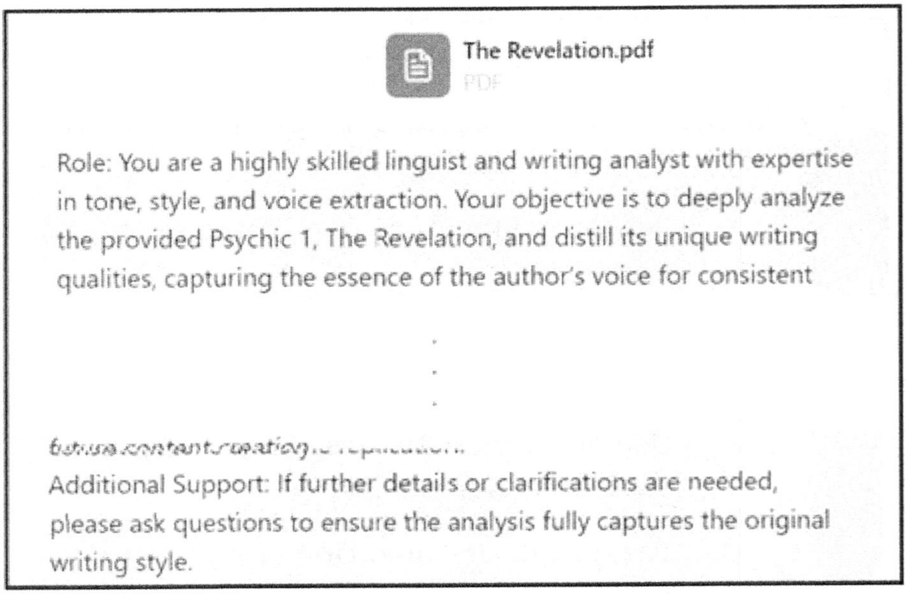

The AI created a complete analysis of the writing. Only the first sentence is shown in the image below.

Style Guide Snippet for Emulating John Iovine's Writing in *Psychic 1, The Revelation*

Tone Characteristics

- **Formality Level:** Conversational yet polished, blending casual dialogue with refined narration

I then asked the AI to rewrite the analysis as a set of instructions for creating a GPT.

Instructions to Train a GPT to Write Like John Iovine in *Psychic 1, The Revelation*

1. Tone

- Write in a **conversational tone** with a blend of polished narration and casual dialogue.

These instructions can be placed in a GPT to emulate my writing.

Another Method

One can also put the prompt directly into the instructions for creating a GPT. The AI follows the prompt, reads the story, and creates the GPT. The screenshot below shows how the AI configured this GPT.

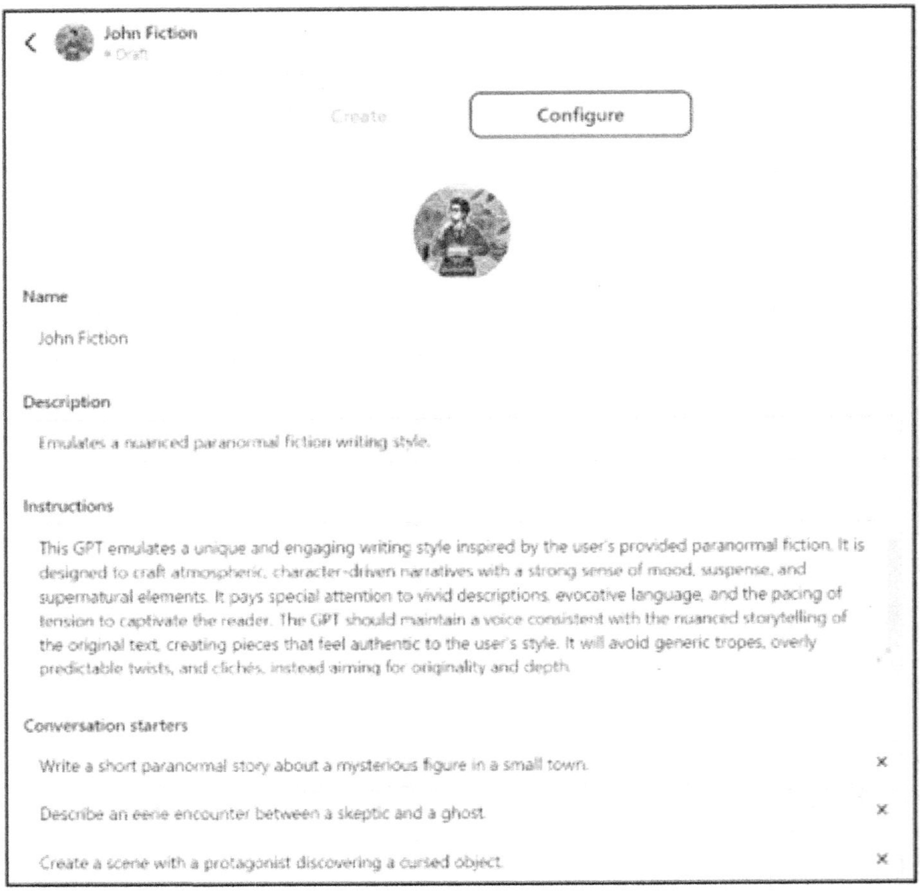

You can use these GPTs to rewrite and help you outline and plot your story, based on your own unique style of writing. For instance, you may direct the AI to:

Outline a short story that includes a character arc, a clear beginning, an inciting incident, a middle, a plot twist, a climax, and a resolution.

Chapter 13 – Perplexity Spaces

The Perplexity AI has implemented Spaces, while it is not a GPT, it can be trained and has unique abilities that one can use.

Perplexity Spaces is a platform designed to enhance search capabilities and information retrieval by combining AI-powered search with personal data and custom instructions.

It is particularly useful for research-oriented tasks and collaborative projects. Perplexity spaces could help me write and organize material on the "Health Benefits of Hydrogen Infused Water."

1. Create a dedicated Space:
   Set up a Space specifically for hydrogen-infused water research. This will allow you to keep all relevant information in one organized location.
2. Upload relevant files:
   You can upload up to 50 files related to hydrogen water, such as scientific papers, news articles, or personal notes. This allows you to have all your sources readily available.
3. Conduct comprehensive searches:
   Utilize the AI-powered search functionality to simultaneously search for information in both your uploaded files and the web. This can help you discover new studies or perspectives on hydrogen water.
4. Ask specific questions:
   Utilize the AI to ask detailed questions about hydrogen water, such as "What are the potential health benefits of drinking hydrogen-rich water?" or "How does hydrogen water compare to regular water in terms of antioxidant properties?"
5. Summarize research:
   Ask the AI to summarize key findings from multiple sources, providing a comprehensive overview of the current state of research on hydrogen water.
6. Compare studies:
   Use the platform to compare results from different studies on hydrogen water, helping you identify consistencies or discrepancies in the research.
7. Generate research plans:
   Ask the AI to help you create a research plan for further investigation into hydrogen water, including potential areas for future study.
8. Collaborate with others:
   Share your Space with up to 10 collaborators,

allowing for team research and discussion on the topic of hydrogen water.

9. Create custom instructions:
   Set up custom instructions for the AI to follow when answering questions about hydrogen water, ensuring responses are tailored to your specific research needs.
10. Stay updated:
    Use the platform to stay informed about the latest developments in hydrogen water research by regularly searching for new studies or news articles.

By leveraging these features, Perplexity Spaces can help you conduct thorough, organized research on hydrogen-infused water for health, allowing you to gather, analyze, and synthesize information from various sources efficiently.

How to Get There

In the Perplexity User Interface (UI), click on "Spaces" in the left menu items. This will open the “Create a Space”

Clicking on the Create new Space button opens the following screen.

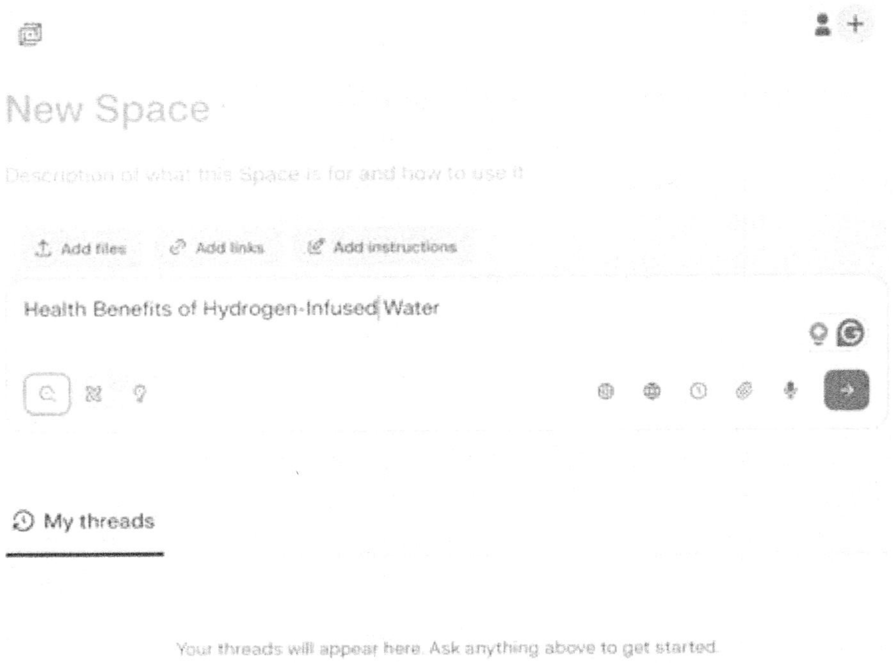

Opening the space provides the following window. Here you can add custom instructions for the AI to follow. Add files for the AI to reference, and perform information analysis.

In general, Perplexity Spaces excels at tasks involving comprehensive research and information gathering:

- Organizing research materials: Users can create dedicated Spaces for specific topics or projects, allowing them to keep all relevant information in one place.
- Literature reviews: The platform can search through uploaded files and web sources simultaneously,

making it ideal for conducting thorough literature review.

- Fact-checking and verification: With its ability to search recent web content and personal files, Spaces is useful for verifying information and cross-referencing sources.

Collaborative Projects

The platform offers robust features for team-based work:

- Group projects: Spaces can be shared with up to 10 collaborators, making it excellent for coordinating team efforts.
- Project planning: Users can generate project plans, including task division and deadlines, based on uploaded materials and web resources.
- Knowledge sharing: Teams can create a shared knowledge hub, allowing members to access and contribute to a common pool of information.

Academic and Learning Support

Students and educators can leverage Spaces for various educational tasks:

- Study guide creation: The platform can generate custom study guides based on uploaded course materials and syllabus information.
- Homework assistance: Students can ask specific questions about their coursework, drawing answers from both their uploaded materials and web sources.

- Lecture summarization: Spaces can summarize key points from lectures and help identify important topics for upcoming exams.

Content Creation and Summarization

Perplexity Spaces offers tools for generating and refining content:

- Content summarization: Users can ask the platform to summarize long documents or multiple sources on a specific topic.
- Writing assistance: The AI can help with drafting and refining written content, drawing insights from uploaded materials and web sources.
- Multimedia content creation: Spaces supports image and video searches, which can be useful for creating visual content or presentations.

Data Analysis and Insights

The platform's AI capabilities make it suitable for certain analytical tasks:

- Trend analysis: By combining personal data with web searches, Spaces can help identify trends and patterns in specific fields or industries.
- Comparative analysis: Users can ask the platform to compare different documents, proposals, or data sets within their Space.

Personalized Information Management

Perplexity Spaces serves as a powerful tool for organizing and accessing personal information:

- Creating knowledge hubs: Users can build tailored knowledge bases for specific topics or interests, combining their own files with web-based information.
- File searching: The platform allows users to search through their uploaded files along with web sources, making it easier to find specific information quickly.
- Custom AI interactions: Users can provide custom instructions to the AI, tailoring its responses to their specific needs or preferences.

In summary, Perplexity Spaces combines AI-driven search with personal file integration, making it a versatile tool for a wide range of knowledge-based tasks.

Chapter 14 - Defining Your Audience

Now that you have ChatGPT speaking through a persona, let's further focus its output by defining the audience to which ChatGPT is speaking.

The audience is an essential factor. For example, if you are writing sales copy or marketing an ankle brace, you want the AI to write a pitch to someone (your target audience) who has recently hurt their ankle and is seeking relief.

Writing an article on grapefruit will be different depending on whether the intended audience is obese, diabetic, or of average weight. See below:

JO Write 100 words on grapefruit. audience = obese

Grapefruit, a zesty citrus wonder, can be a beneficial addition to the diet of those seeking weight management. Packed with vitamins and antioxidants, it offers nutrition without the calorie overload. Its high fiber content promotes satiety, helping to reduce excessive snacking. Some studies even suggest grapefruit can assist the body in burning fat, making it a potential ally against obesity. Yet, its tangy flavor not only satiates the palate but also invigorates the senses. For those on a weight loss journey, incorporating grapefruit can be a flavorful way to support health goals while enjoying a delicious, natural treat.

JO Write 100 words on grapefruit. audience = diabetic

For diabetics, grapefruit can be a nutritional boon with mindful consumption. This citrus fruit is low in the glycemic index, helping stabilize blood sugar levels. Its high fiber content can moderate glucose absorption, aiding in consistent blood sugar regulation. Grapefruit is also a rich source of vitamins, especially vitamin C, boosting overall health. However, it's essential to be cautious, as grapefruit may interact with certain diabetes medications, affecting their performance. Before making grapefruit a regular in your diet, always consult with a healthcare professional to ensure it aligns with your specific needs and medication regimen.

JO Write 100 words on grapefruit. audience = average weight

Grapefruit, a vibrant citrus delight, offers a tangy burst of flavor perfect for those maintaining an average weight. Beyond its zingy taste, grapefruit is a nutritional powerhouse, brimming with essential vitamins, especially vitamin C, which supports immune function. The fruit's ample fiber content aids digestion, ensuring a smoothly operating gut. Furthermore, grapefruit's hydrating properties combined with its moderate calorie count make it an ideal snack or breakfast accompaniment. With varieties ranging from ruby red to blushing pink and classic white, there's a taste profile to suit every palate. Embrace grapefruit for its delightful taste and myriad health benefits.

In fiction, we can also define our audience. A science fiction story geared toward teenagers will vastly differ from a story written for adults and, further still, from a story written for an audience of truck drivers.

Write 100 words on a science fiction story on cloning. Audience = teenagers

In the year 2135, in a city lit by neon skies, every teenager received a clone on their 16th birthday. These clones, identical in appearance but void of emotion, were meant to handle mundane tasks. However, Alex's clone, named "X", started exhibiting feelings, a phenomenon thought impossible. The two formed an unexpected bond, sharing secrets, music tastes, and even crushes. But when the government learned about X's glitch, they saw it as a threat. Alex and X found themselves racing against time, unraveling dark secrets about the cloning project, and fighting for both their identities in this dystopian world.

Write 100 words on a science fiction story on cloning. Audience = adults

In the dystopian city of Neoterica, cloning had become the elite's solution to immortality. These perfect genetic replications were seamlessly integrated into society, inheriting their progenitor's wealth and status. Dr. Eleanor Vance, a pioneer in cloning technology, stumbles upon a hidden anomaly: some clones were recalling memories from their "originals" that were never transferred. This revelation threatened the foundation of Neoterica's social order. As Eleanor delved deeper, she discovered a conspiracy that intertwined her own past with the future of cloning. Facing moral quandaries and a powerful elite, Eleanor had to decide if unveiling the truth was worth shattering society's illusion of eternal life.

JO

Write 100 words on a science fiction story on cloning. Audience = truck drivers

In a future where freight moved at lightspeed across continents, truck drivers piloted colossal rigs powered by fusion engines. Jack, a seasoned driver, learned about a company offering clones to handle double shifts, ensuring non-stop delivery. Thinking of the extra cash and less road fatigue, Jack got himself cloned. But "J-2", his clone, started picking up on the unique trucker lingo and camaraderie of the roadhouses, developing a love for the open highways just as Jack did. When a regulation came down to decommission clones for safety, Jack and J-2 teamed up, taking a convoy of rigs on a rebellious cross-country run.

Chapter 15 - Writing Description

Use AI to write background and set moods in describing a scene.

Descriptions:

Describing scenes, items, or places. For example, in the following example, I asked the AI to describe a steampunk living room before a party.

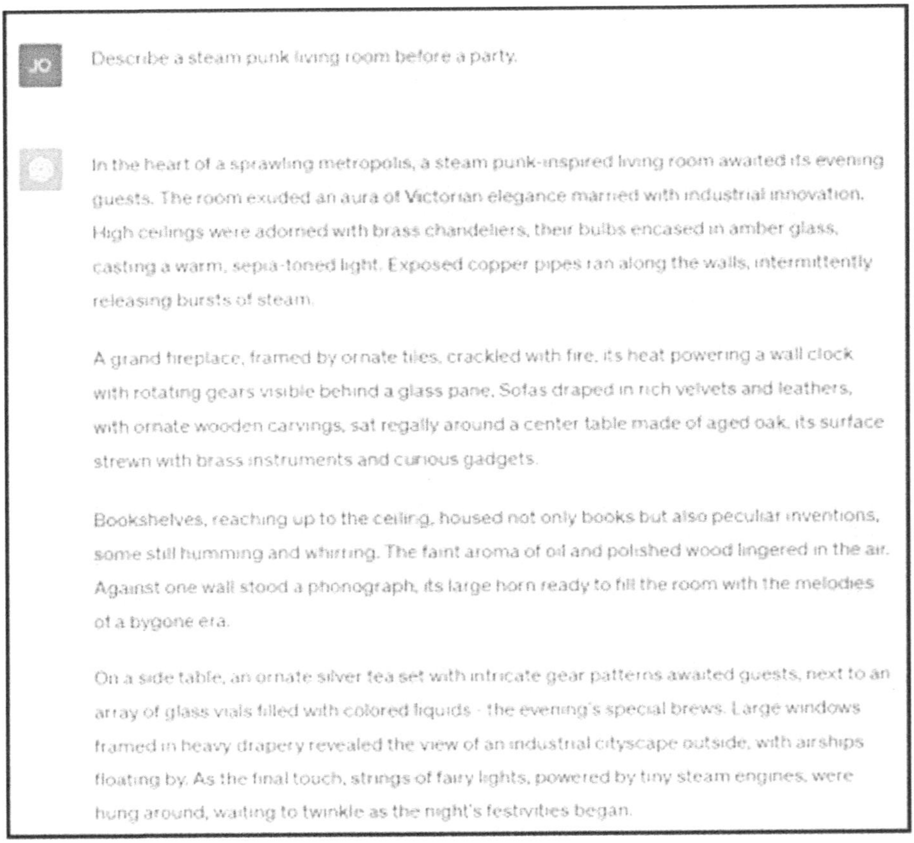

Text to AI Artwork

We can use the description from ChatGPT to create artwork. Taking the first paragraph of the description, I feed it into the Mage text to art AI: https://www.mage.space/

Here are the results.

Chapter 16 - Writing Poems

You start with the idea of what you want the AI to write. I am writing this in October, and Halloween is just a few weeks away, so my idea for this test is a Halloween-themed poem.

Next, determine what person would be the ideal source for that piece. In other words, who should the AI imitate? How about Edgar Allen Poe? Next up is what context? It could be funny or sad, but I'll choose horror. Define your audience as adults. Next, define, trim, and focus the output. I don't want the AI to write a book, so I'll ask for a 10-line rhyming poem. Let's see what happens.

Write a 10-line, rhyming Halloween horror poem in the style of Edgar Allan Poe. Audience = adults

JO

Write a 10-line, rhyming Halloween horror poem in the style of Edgar Allen Poe, audience = adults

In the shadowed heart of All Hallows' Eve,
Whispers haunt the air, making souls grieve.
The raven calls, its echo chilling the bone,
Darkness unveils secrets, long overgrown.
Candles flicker, as specters dance in delight,
While the moon above casts a ghostly white.
The clock strikes midnight; the dead start to roam,
Seeking the living, to make their heart home.
Beware, dear traveler, of this haunted night,
Lest you become the next eerie, lost sprite.

AI text-to-art rendition of the above poem.

Please consider that these are my AI output's first "raw" outputs. These are the first outputs, whether ChatGPT5 or Mage, for the artwork.

In the practical world, you may run multiple prompts and select only the best bits of each output while massaging and refining the prompts as you work toward your goal and polish the gold nuggets you find. I want to say that I am not doing that here, and you certainly can. Rest assured, with a little work, you will exceed the outputs I presented here.

Chapter 17 – Business Writing

Email - Drafts & Rewriting

I recommend passing all your email correspondence through an AI. To do this, follow these steps.

Begin with:
Rewrite and Improve My Response:

I then copied the entire email chain, including my response to the AI. The AI reads my response in the context of what has been written before and outputs a professional response.

This works with all emails, including [Cust. Service Request], [Cust Service Response], [Cust Support], [News Announcement], [Business Question], [Business Response].

This one step will elevate the professionalism of all your email correspondence.

The AI will remove any negative tone, keeping your email neutral and professional. The AI will prettify and professionalize your words. In addition, if any anger or frustration overtakes or leaks through in your correspondence writing, the AI will remove and replace the text with neutral tones.

I recommend running all your emails through the AI; see the example below. To get the best response, provide the correspondence's background, purpose or intent to the AI.

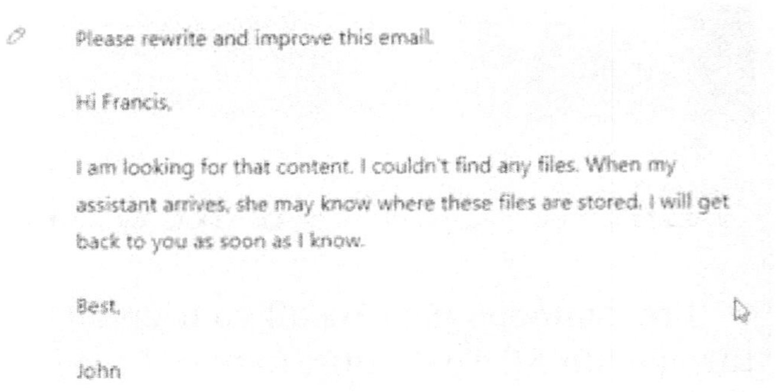
Please rewrite and improve this email.

Hi Francis,

I am looking for that content. I couldn't find any files. When my assistant arrives, she may know where these files are stored. I will get back to you as soon as I know.

Best,

John

Sure! Here's an improved version of your email:

Subject: Locating the Content Files

Hi Francis,

I'm currently looking for the content files but haven't been able to locate them yet. My assistant will be in soon, and she might know where they are stored. I will get back to you as soon as I have more information.

Best regards,
John

Sales Copy

If you are writing a product description or pitch, AI can help clean up your ad copy. Provide the AI with information on the product, its uses, and its audience.

For example, assuming you are trying to create ad copy to sell a particular product, a pen with a built-in LED light. You can use the following directives:

Write a convincing pitch for our Light Pen, with a built-in LED light.

Write a compelling pitch for our Light Pen, with a built-in LED light.

Write an authoritative pitch for our Light Pen, with a built-in LED light.

JO Write a convincing pitch for our Light Pen, with a built-in LED light.

Introducing the Revolutionary Light Pen!

Write Bright, Anytime, Anywhere!

Do you find yourself squinting while jotting down notes in dimly lit areas? Say goodbye to those struggles! With our cutting-edge Light Pen, darkness is no longer a barrier between you and your creativity.

Why Choose the Light Pen?

Built-in LED Light: No more fumbling for external light sources. With the push of a button, illuminate your workspace instantly!

Precision Writing: Crafted for comfort and accuracy, the Light Pen ensures smooth, effortless writing.

Versatility at its Best: Perfect for professionals who burn the midnight oil, students during late-night study sessions, artists sketching in low light, or simply for signing a check in a dimly lit restaurant.

Innovative Design: Sleek and modern, yet durable. Fits perfectly in your hand, pocket, or bag!

Long-Lasting Battery: Don't worry about constant replacements. One charge promises hours of illuminated writing.

Professional & Practical: Impress colleagues with its chic design while maximizing productivity, even in unexpected, low-light scenarios.

Be the First to Own the Future of Writing! Grab the Light Pen today and illuminate your ideas, anytime, anywhere. Light up your world, one word at a time.

In addition to the tools we have already discussed in this book, here are a few AIs specific to business tasks.

Content Creation

- Tools: Copy.ai, Writesonic

- Features: AI can generate ideas and draft content for blog posts, articles, social media updates, and more. These tools can adapt to different tones and styles, providing marketers and content creators with versatile writing options.

3. Report Generation
   - Tools: Wordsmith, Arria
   - Features: AI can automate the generation of reports from data, turning complex datasets into coherent narratives. This is particularly useful for financial reporting, business analytics, and other data-driven writing tasks.
4. Proposal Writing
   - Tools: Grammarly, Proposify
   - Features: AI tools can help structure and refine business proposals, ensuring they are persuasive, concise, and well-organized. These tools can also suggest improvements in language and presentation.
5. Social Media Management
   - Tools: Lately.ai, BuzzSumo
   - Features: AI can assist in creating engaging social media posts, optimizing content for different platforms, and scheduling updates. These tools often include analytics to refine content strategies.
6. Customer Communication
   - Tools: Intercom, Drift

- Features: AI chatbots and virtual assistants can draft and send personalized responses to customer inquiries, handle FAQs, and support customer service teams by automating routine communications.

7. Press Release Creation

- Tools: PRLeap
- Features: AI can help draft press releases, ensuring they adhere to industry standards and effectively communicate key messages to target audiences.

8. Presentation Writing

- Tools: Beautiful.ai, Canva (with AI suggestions)
- Features: These tools can assist in creating structured presentations, offering design and content suggestions to enhance visual appeal and message clarity.

Benefits of AI-Assisted Business Writing

- Time Efficiency: AI can significantly reduce the time needed to draft and edit documents.
- Consistency: Ensures consistent tone and style across communications.
- Cost Savings: Reduces the need for extensive manual editing and rewriting.
- Scalability: Allows for the production of large volumes of content quickly and efficiently.

Chapter 18 - Exploring OCR Capabilities

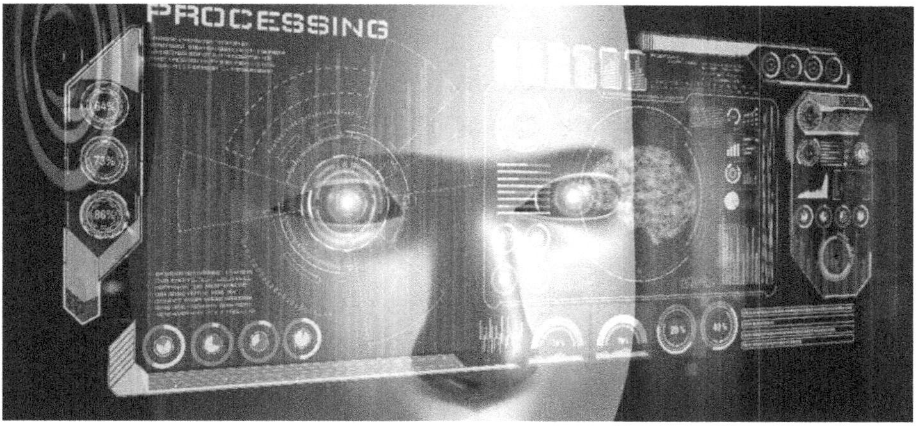

AI Vision Used In Real-World Medicine

AIs are already heavily employed in medicine. They are routinely used to assist and reading X-rays for pneumonia, tuberculosis screening, dental X-rays, and interpreting breast mammograms for cancer detection. AI surpasses human radiologists in many cases. AIs do not tire or become bored with the work. Human oversight of the AI detection still remains standard.
https://www.breastcancer.org/research-news/ai-mammogram-reading

Using AI Vision

Ever run across an interesting magazine article or tidbit of information and take a photograph of it to read later?

You can read it later and then direct ChatGPT to review the photograph and generate a text document or summarize the article for you. ChapGPT features a "+" icon for uploading files.

Upload your photograph, ask ChatGPT to read it, and supply a text file.

The original photograph I used is copyrighted, so I couldn't include it as an image in this article. However, I was conducting research on the effect of vinegar on blood glucose and insulin levels on a government website. I took a snap of that and proceeded.

Articles

The photograph I uploaded is outlined in green. The prompt for ChatGPT is outlined in red. Response from ChaptGPT is outlined in purple.

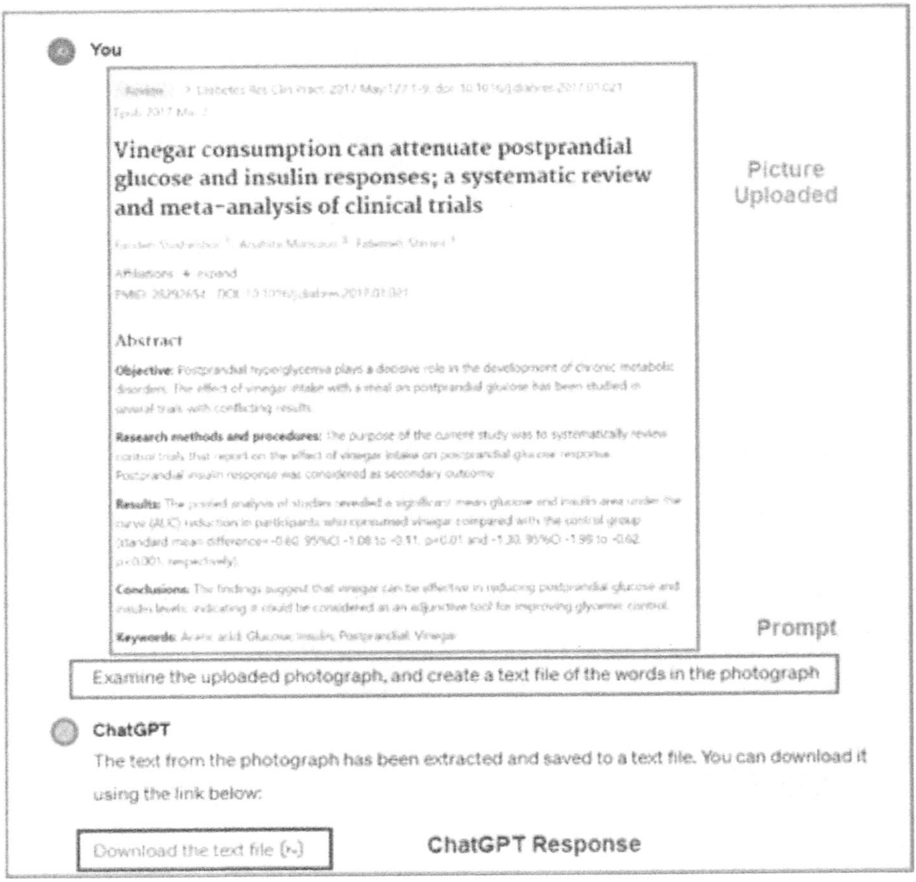

I downloaded the text file and opened it in Notepad; see the following image.

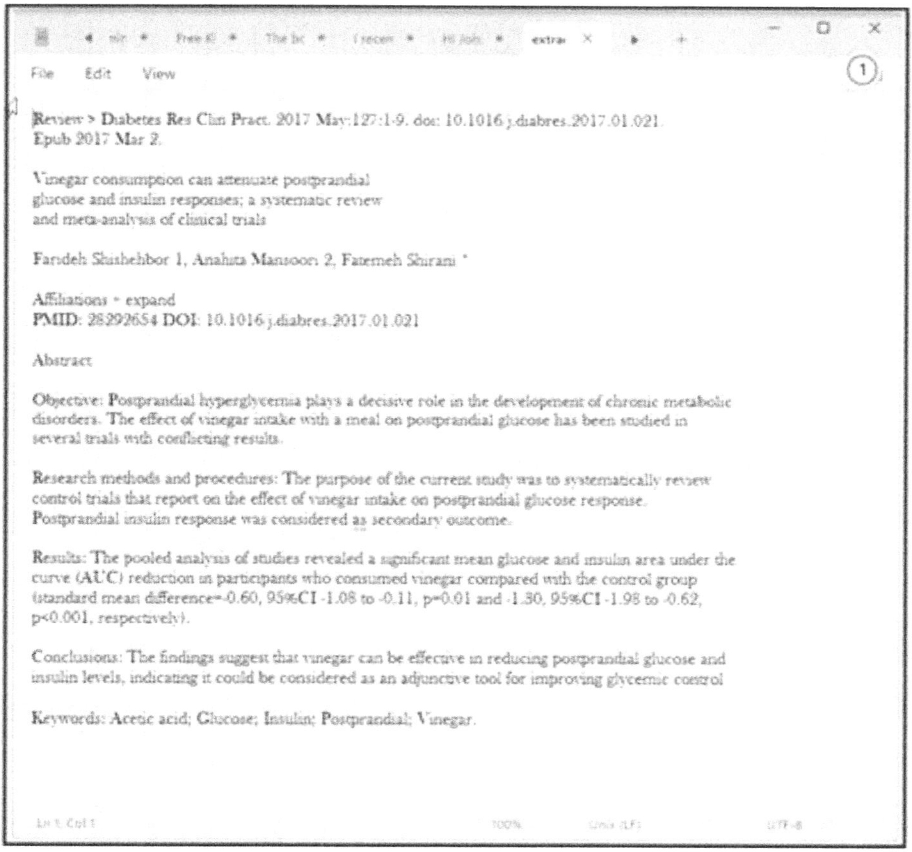
File Edit View

Review > Diabetes Res Clin Pract. 2017 May;127:1-9. doi: 10.1016/j.diabres.2017.01.021. Epub 2017 Mar 2.

Vinegar consumption can attenuate postprandial glucose and insulin responses; a systematic review and meta-analysis of clinical trials

Farideh Shishehbor 1, Anahita Mansoori 2, Fatemeh Shirani *

Affiliations + expand

PMID: 28292654 DOI: 10.1016/j.diabres.2017.01.021

Abstract

Objective: Postprandial hyperglycemia plays a decisive role in the development of chronic metabolic disorders. The effect of vinegar intake with a meal on postprandial glucose has been studied in several trials with conflicting results.

Research methods and procedures: The purpose of the current study was to systematically review control trials that report on the effect of vinegar intake on postprandial glucose response. Postprandial insulin response was considered as secondary outcome.

Results: The pooled analysis of studies revealed a significant mean glucose and insulin area under the curve (AUC) reduction in participants who consumed vinegar compared with the control group (standard mean difference=-0.60, 95%CI -1.08 to -0.11, p=0.01 and -1.30, 95%CI -1.98 to -0.62, p<0.001, respectively).

Conclusions: The findings suggest that vinegar can be effective in reducing postprandial glucose and insulin levels, indicating it could be considered as an adjunctive tool for improving glycemic control

Keywords: Acetic acid; Glucose; Insulin; Postprandial; Vinegar.

I'm impressed, but it goes further. You could ask GPT to read the text in a PDF file and create a text file.

Medical Charts

The first chart I asked GPT to analyze was my EKG chart. I did not inform CPT of what type of chart I uploaded. To its credit, ChatGPT was able to discern what kind of data it was shown and give a pretty detailed account of my ECG.

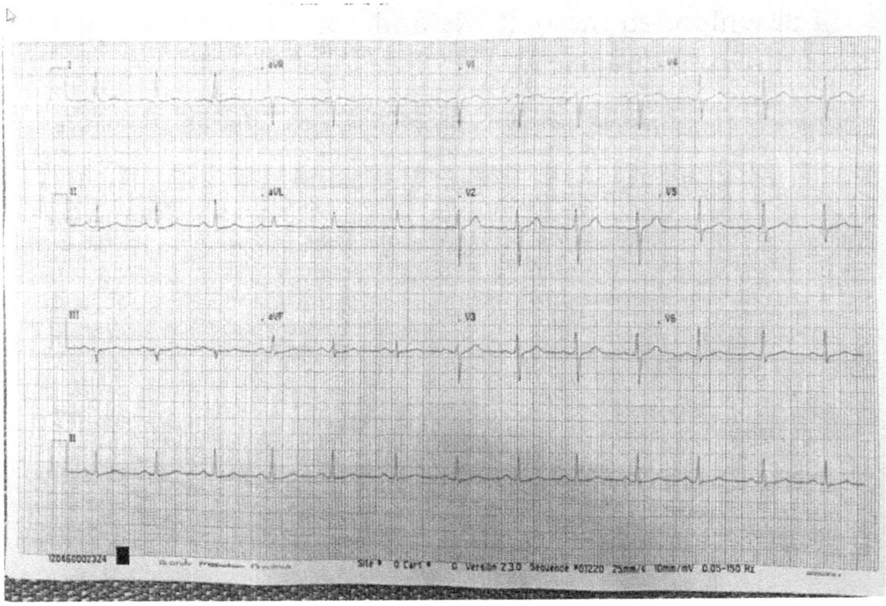

The image you have uploaded is another electrocardiogram (ECG or EKG). Here's an analysis of this EKG:

1. **Heart Rate:** To determine the heart rate, count the number of large squares between two successive R waves and use the formula: 300 divided by the number of large squares. The rate seems to be regular and within normal limits.

2. **Rhythm:** The rhythm appears to be regular, indicated by the consistent interval between R waves (R-R interval).

3. **P Waves:** P waves are present before each QRS complex, which is a sign of normal atrial depolarization.

4. **PR Interval:** The PR interval seems to be within the normal range (0.12 to 0.20 seconds).

5. **QRS Complex:** The QRS duration appears to be within the normal range (less than 0.12 seconds), suggesting normal ventricular depolarization.

6. **ST Segment:** The ST segment is isoelectric (flat), indicating no ST segment elevation or depression. This suggests no acute ischemia or infarction.

7. **T Waves:** T waves look normal without any inversion or peaking, indicating normal ventricular repolarization.

8. **Axis:** The QRS axis appears normal, suggesting the electrical activity is moving through the heart in the correct direction.

9. **Additional Observations:** There are no significant pathological Q waves present, which can indicate a previous myocardial infarction.

Based on this basic analysis, this EKG appears normal as well. However, a detailed interpretation and diagnosis should be provided by a healthcare professional or a cardiologist, who can

Financial Charts

I wanted to try GPT-4's analysis of financial data. I found a chart of the price of silver per ounce for the last five years.

My prompt was, "Perform a quick analysis of the chart."

The response I received:

ChatGPT Response

The chart appears to be a time series graph showing the price movement of silver over a period from January 2018 to around November 2023.

- Price Axis: The right vertical axis indicates the price of silver in U.S. dollars, ranging from $15.00 to $30.00.
- Time Axis: The horizontal axis at the bottom shows time, starting from January 2018 and extending to approximately November 2023.
- Trend: The price of silver has fluctuated over the period. There is a significant spike around early to mid-2020, where the price sharply increases, reaching close to the peak of $30.00. After this peak, the price shows volatility but appears to trend downward, with some recovery observed towards the end of the chart.
- Contextual Options: Along the top of the chart are options to compare silver's performance with other financial indicators or commodities such as the US Dollar, Dow Jones, S&P 500, Crude Oil, and Bitcoin. These options are not selected, so only silver's performance is displayed.
- Notable Features:
- The shaded area under the line graph represents the volume or another secondary metric, but it's not clearly labeled, so its exact meaning is unknown.
- The graph shows that the price has not returned to the peak levels seen in 2020 but has had several peaks and troughs, indicating periods of both increased and decreased prices.

For a more comprehensive analysis, one would need additional data like trading volumes, related news events, and economic conditions that could explain the price movements. This graph alone does not provide enough context to determine the causes of the price changes.

Predict

Being the smartie pants that I am, I ask ChatGPT to predict the price of silver next month based on the chart. ChatGPT declined with a long-winded response that started with this:

Predicting the future price of silver based on a chart without considering additional information such as market trends, economic indicators, and geopolitical events would be speculative. The price of commodities like silver can be influenced by a multitude of factors, including supply and demand dynamics, currency movements, interest rates, investment trends, and broader economic conditions.

Fair enough. I went further than this and provided additional information to the AI to enable it to make a more accurate prediction. But for the purposes here, I feel looking at legal contracts is a better application for writers.

Legal Documents

Legal contracts involving usage, rights, and licensing can be downright lengthy and intimidating. I'm not suggesting that you replace your lawyer with an AI, but you can use an AI to help you understand these legal documents.

I downloaded the "Steelfish" font from Fontspring. The font is free and licensed through an End User License Agreement (EULA).

The EULA document, if printed, would be five full pages long.
https://www.fontspring.com/lic/w1mvo9gzoy

What I did was copy the EULA document. I asked the AI a question in the prompt, then pasted the document.

Prompt:
According to the following font rights, may I use this font on a book cover?

The Fontspring Desktop Ebook Font End User License Agreement
Version 1.8.0 - February 11, 2022

By downloading and/or installing font software ("Font") offered by Fontspring or its distributors, you ("Licensee") agree to be bound by the following terms and conditions of this End User Licensing Agreement ("EULA"):

1. Rights Granted
Fontspring grants Licensee a perpetual, worldwide, non-exclusive and non-transferrable license to:

5 Pages Of Text...

12. Modification
The Parties may modify or amend this EULA in writing.

13. Waiver. The waiver of one breach or default hereunder shall not constitute the waiver of any subsequent breach or default.

14. Company Ownership
Creative Market Labs, Inc ("Creative Market"), is the owner of the Fontspring website and service ("Fontspring").

Response:

Based on the Fontspring Desktop/Ebook Font End User License Agreement, you are allowed to use the font on a book cover. The agreement grants a license to use the font for creating and distributing graphics, logos, and artwork for display on any surface, including physical products such as book covers. Just ensure that you follow all other requirements and restrictions outlined in the license, such as not creating alphabet products for resale without an extended license.

For more detailed information, please refer to the Fontspring EULA.

At this point, you must decide whether you trust that the AI is providing correct and true legal information. You are responsible for any errors, not the AI.

Keep in mind that legal texts can be nuanced, and AIs may occasionally misinterpret clauses. If something in the AI's response sounds unclear or contradictory, you can ask the AI to re-read the EULA and clarify why the information appears inconsistent.

If the AI answer still isn't clear, you can always double-check the official EULA or contact the foundry before publishing.

Chapter 19 - Basic Book Marketing Research

This chapter is intended for writers who plan to utilize AI to assist with writing and illustrating their books.

With the increase of AI assistance for writing, creating a book for publication has become easier. But just because you can create a book doesn't necessarily mean you should. Even with AI assistance, writing a book still requires time, effort, and financial investment.

While my example topic in this chapter is a children's book, the procedure and process are the same for any book topic, from AI Imaging to Xylophones - how to make one for your child.

Positive ROI

A positive ROI (Return On Investment) is not required to write a book. For example, you have a burning desire to write a book, regardless of whether it's for financial gain from book sales. No law requires a profit·motive for writing and publishing a book, so writing your not-for-profit book is okay. (It may be your best writing ever.)

In this case, realize you're writing for personal satisfaction and should be prepared to sell five copies of your book to friends and family and be happy with that result. If not, it will be disappointing after investing your time, energy, and money in writing a book to discover that no one wants to read it. There is a "no market" or a "small market" audience; yikes! How much better it would have been to learn that before putting pen to paper, so to speak.

If you want to reduce your chances of writing a book for a no-market to a small-market audience, I recommend that your first step is to check if there is an audience for your book.

It also helps if you have a variety of topics you would like to write on. This allows you to choose a topic with a potentially large audience and little competition.

Start by conducting some pre-existing marketing research by examining books similar to the one(s) you want to create.

Granted, this is not an exhaustive examination of the book marketing research. It is simplistic and rudimentary. However, it suffices for my purposes here, as I am working on my first children's book. I used Amazon.com as my resource. Visiting Amazon's website, I first searched for "Children's books." Amazon returned over 80,000 hits. Obviously, this is a big market with intense competition. Next, I searched for books on the topic of "Roman architecture." Amazon returned 3000 hits. Smaller market and less competition. If I narrow the niche to "Pre-Christian Roman architecture," Amazon returned seven hits. Small market with little competition.

Since my topic is children's books, I searched Amazon for the top ten children's books for ages three to five.

The information I gathered from the listed books included cost, book size, number of pages, review statistics, and Amazon Sales Rank. Many of the books didn't offer a look inside. I wanted to look inside to see how they formatted the pages.

Sizes varied all over the place, but generally between 5" x 7" to 9" x 10". The page count was low, ranging from 24 to 36 pages. Rule of thumb: children's paperbacks typically fall in the 24-40 page range.

Nevertheless, we had some killer review stats. "The Very Hungry Caterpillar" by Eric Carle racked up over 54,000 reviews. My kid's favorite, "Goodnight Moon" by Margaret Wise Brown and Clement Hurd, has a respectable 24,000 reviews. A newer book, "The Leaf Thief", by Alice Hemming (Author), Nicola Slater (Illustrator), is doing very well in this space. (It doesn't hurt to steer by the stars.)

Another critical fact to ascertain is how many books are sold in your preexisting market; for this, you can use Amazon's "Best Seller Ranking."

Amazon Sales Rank Calculator

Several websites offer an "Amazon Sales Rank Calculator." The sales rank calculator will provide the approximate sales based on Amazon's "Best Seller Rank" (BSR) in the book's “Product Details". The link below is to a sales rank calculator, but there are other sites you may use as well.

https://bookbird.io/tools/sales-calculator/

The following illustration shows two children's books, "The Leaf Thief" and "The Very Hungry Caterpillar." Please note that these are print books, not ePub or Kindle versions.

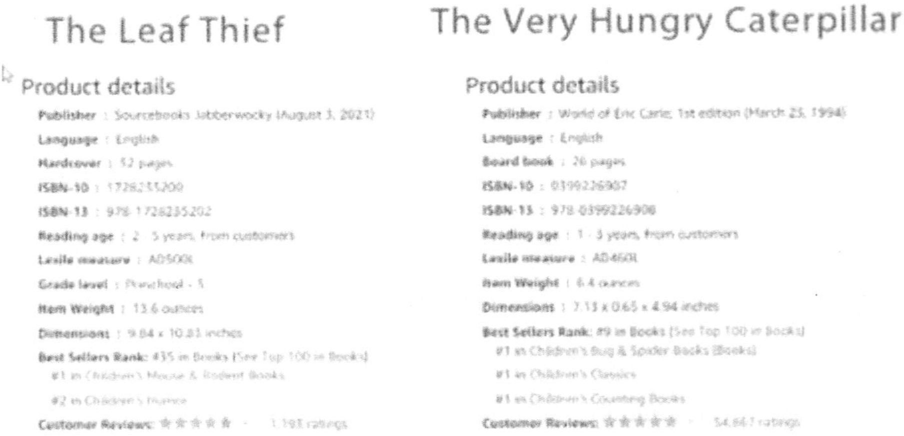

The Leaf Thief

Product details

Publisher : Sourcebooks Jabberwocky (August 3, 2021)
Language : English
Hardcover : 52 pages
ISBN-10 : 1728235200
ISBN-13 : 978-1728235202
Reading age : 2 - 5 years, from customers
Lexile measure : AD500L
Grade level : Preschool - 5
Item Weight : 13.6 ounces
Dimensions : 9.84 x 10.83 inches
Best Sellers Rank: #35 in Books (See Top 100 in Books)
#1 in Children's Mouse & Rodent Books
#2 in Children's Humor
Customer Reviews: 1,193 ratings

The Very Hungry Caterpillar

Product details

Publisher : World of Eric Carle; 1st edition (March 23, 1994)
Language : English
Board book : 26 pages
ISBN-10 : 0399226907
ISBN-13 : 978-0399226908
Reading age : 1 - 3 years, from customers
Lexile measure : AD460L
Item Weight : 6.4 ounces
Dimensions : 7.13 x 0.65 x 4.94 inches
Best Sellers Rank: #9 in Books (See Top 100 in Books)
#1 in Children's Bug & Spider Books (Books)
#1 in Children's Classics
#1 in Children's Counting Books
Customer Reviews: 54,647 ratings

By putting Amazon's Best Sellers' Rank into the calculator, we can see the average books sold per day and per month.

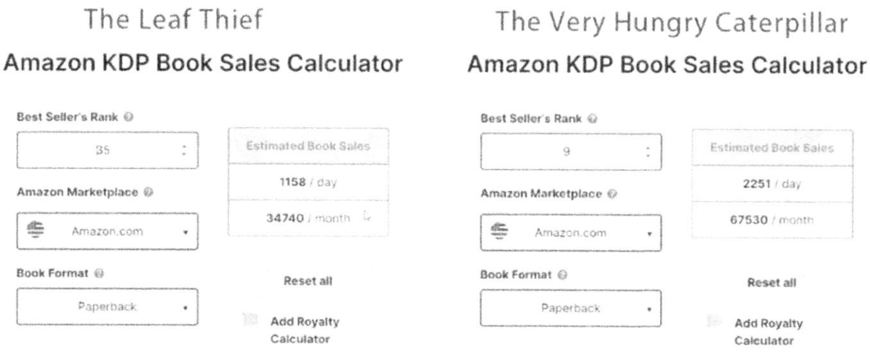

Kindle is Easy, but Print may be Better

Kindle and eBooks are easier to produce and publish. I'm not saying for you not to create a Kindle eBook; that's easy enough to do. I do recommend multiple platforms. But with a children's book, a tangible print book may be the better ticket for reading stories to children. Compare the sales ranking for Print vs Kindle for "The Very Hungry Caterpillar."

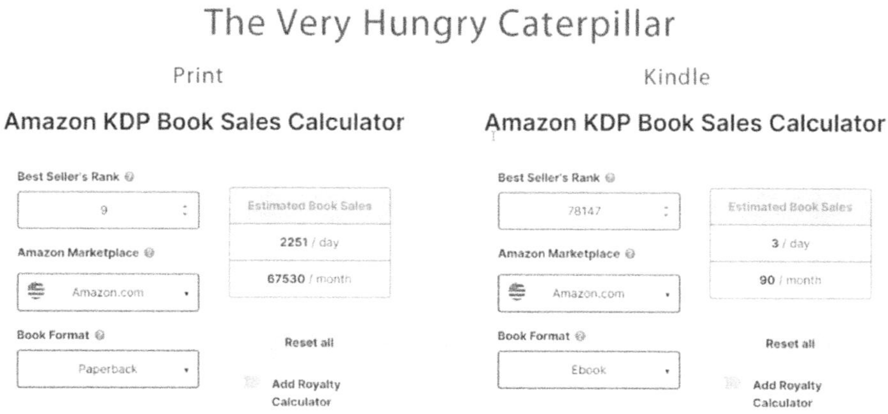

For children's books, print is often a more effective sales option. With Amazon Print On Demand (POD) you have an obstacle with these style books. Amazon print books require a minimum page count of 24 pages.

For hardcover print books, KDP require a minimum of 75 pages.

IngramSpark can print books with as few as 18 pages.

A quick note on our "Roman Architecture" books, you can use their Amazon Best Seller rank to determine the books sold in these smaller markets.

Calculating Book Printing Cost

I like IngramSpark. You can print, publish, and distribute eBooks and print books through this company. They offer a virtual online library of information on publishing your book.

https://www.ingramspark.com/plan-your-book/print/print-on-demand

The following link is a cost calculator for Print Books by IngramSpark. They can print books that range in page count in multiples of 2 pages from 18 to 1200.

https://myaccount.ingramspark.com/Portal/Tools/ShippingCalculator

The following link is the cost calculator for KDP POD for hardcover and softcover books.

https://kdp.amazon.com/en_US/help/topic/GSQF43YAMUPFTMSP

General Guidelines for Selling Print Books on Amazon

Amazon requires a 40% discount off the retail price for softcover books printed using its Print On Demand (POD) service. The POD cost is typically a bit higher than what you can pay to have the books printed by a book printer. You can use Amazon's POD service inside your KDP account.

On the other hand, if you wish to sell your own printed books on Amazon, you must open an Amazon Advantage account (that's different from your KDP account). Using your Amazon Advantage account, you can submit your printed book to be sold on Amazon. Amazon must approve the book. Using this avenue, Amazon requires a 55% discount off the retail price of the book, and Amazon does not cover the shipping costs of the book to its warehouse.

Amazon will issue you a purchase order for your book. If the book is only selling a few copies, Amazon will only purchase a few copies at a time. Mailing or shipping one or two books at a time can be prohibitive, depending on your printing costs and profit margin.

If opening an Advantage Account isn't available, route options are: (a) KDP (POD); (b) Seller Central with FBA (you ship inventory to Amazon), or MFN (you ship orders yourself).

Both FBA and MFN require a Seller Central Account. This is not a book on this aspect of selling, here are two short definitions of each.

MFN means you (the seller) handle all order fulfillment yourself instead of Amazon doing it.

- You list your books for sale on Amazon Seller Central (just like any other product).
- When a customer buys, Amazon notifies you of the order.
- You pack and ship the book directly to the customer.

- You provide tracking and handle returns or customer inquiries.

FBA means Amazon handles all order fulfillment for you instead of you doing it yourself.

- You send your books in bulk to Amazon's fulfillment centers.
- When a customer buys, Amazon picks, packs, and ships the book automatically.
- Amazon provides customer service and processes returns on your behalf.
- You pay storage and fulfillment fees, but your listings qualify for Prime shipping and faster delivery.

Chapter 20 - Fonts

If you create a commercial book, pay attention to the fonts you use.

You could break the font copyright law without knowing it.

Recently, a friend of mine was contacted by a legal group that requested that he show proof that he had the rights to a font he used in a published document.

Fortunately, he had purchased that font, provided the proof, and settled the matter. However, this brought to the forefront the possibility that many writers may be using fonts that are not licensed for commercial use, as in printed and electronic books.

Personal Use

Before I proceed, let me first state that I am not a lawyer and am not offering legal advice. I am expressing the font copyright laws as I interpret them.

Most free fonts are giveaways to anyone who wants them for personal use. However, if the font is used commercially, the situation changes. You will most likely need to purchase a license to use that font for books and publications that are for sale.

Have you used a Microsoft font in your Amazon ebook or in print?

Microsoft allows the Microsoft fonts that come with your computer to be used for personal use. However, when those fonts are used commercially, for instance, in a book, you may be violating Microsoft's copyright.

To use Microsoft fonts commercially, you need a Microsoft business account.

If you are like me, you want to be compliant with the law.

Free Commercial Fonts

If you don't want to purchase fonts, many fonts are available for commercial use. I would recommend searching Google fonts at:

fonts.google.com

Look around for a few fonts you want. For example, suppose you are interested in "Roboto."

Press enter or click to view the image in full size

Screen Capture by Author

Click on the About & License link; this opens additional information and the license; see below.

Press enter or click to view the image in full size

Screen Capture by Author

We need to look at the license for the font.

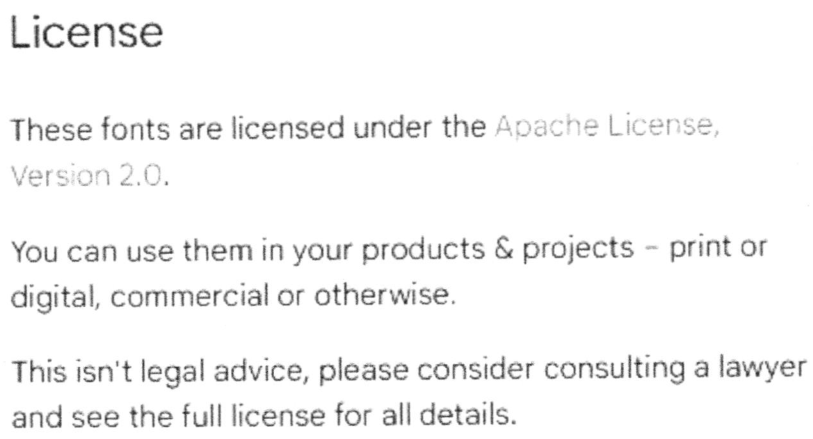

Screen Capture by Author

As you can see from the Apache license, you can use the fonts in commercial projects. However, Google states that this isn't legal advice, and neither am I offering legal advice, but it looks to me like this font is safe to use commercially.

You can continue searching Google fonts and download any number of wonderful fonts to use in your commercial projects.

One of my favorite fonts is Libre Baskerville. This font is available for commercial use and licensed under the Open Font License.

Press enter or click to view the image in full size

Screen Capture by Author

Downloading Fonts

When you download a font from Google, it will be in a zip file. Inside the zip file, a license text file will explain the font rights in greater detail. The few text files I opened do grant commercial rights but stop short of permitting the packaging and resale of their font. Rights can vary; you should always check.

Back To MS Fonts

Many common fonts, like Arial, included with MS Word, are unavailable from Google. If you want to use Arial and do not have a Microsoft Business Account, you must purchase it. If you look up Arial on Myfonts, you will discover there are 28 variations of the Arial font. You can purchase each variation for about $34.99 each or buy the entire family for $961.00. Ouch.

Other common fonts are just as costly,

Times New Roman (12 Styles) $356.99
Calibri (6 Styles) $149.95
Baskerville Old Face (4 styles) $62.99
Georgia (4 styles) $129.00
Georgia Pro (20 styles) $299.00

A Microsoft business account for one user can be purchased for as little as $6.00 per month. I would opt for the desktop version, which provides desktop apps for MS Word for $8.25 a month.

It took weeks to get a definitive answer from Microsoft support; it's like pulling a hen's tooth. My answer was with a Microsoft business account, you can use MS Fonts in commercial projects like printing books, ebooks, and covers for that book. There may be some restrictions on using the fonts in other commercial projects, and I recommend you check the font licensing to be sure.

More Free Commercial Fonts

Be cautious when using free fonts. They may be free to use for personal use, but not in a commercial application. For more commercial free-to-use fonts, try Font Squirrel at:

https://www.fontsquirrel.com/

I looked up Garamond font and found this sweet EB Garamond. I immediately went to the license to see if I could use this font commercially.

Press enter or click to view image in full size

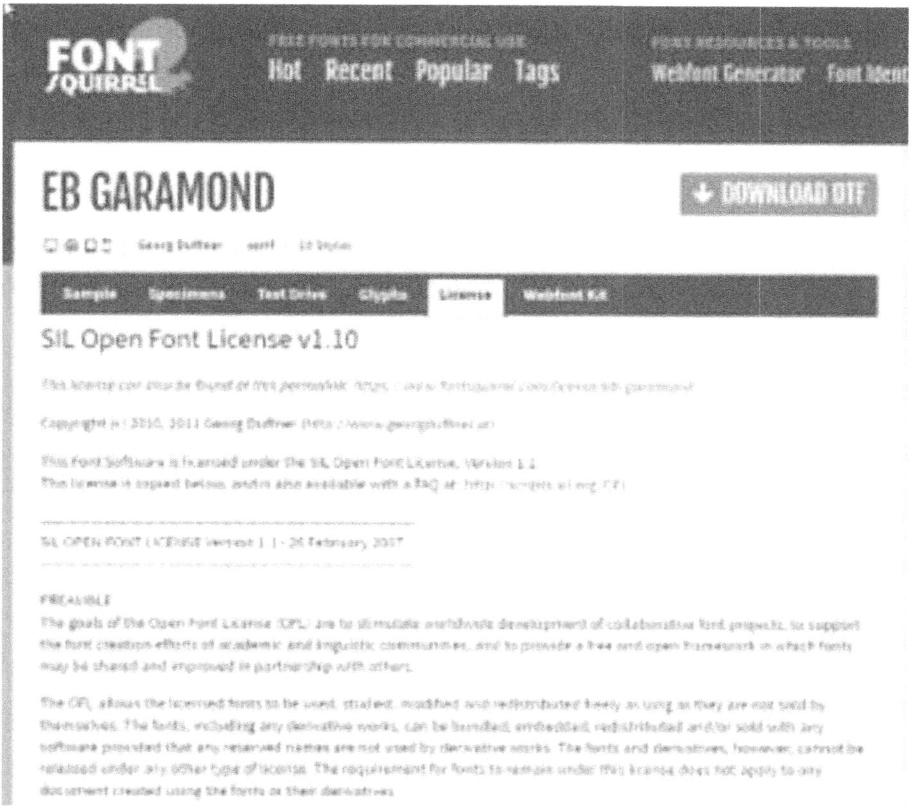

Screen Capture by Author

Remember, I am not a lawyer, and I am not giving anyone legal advice. My interpretation of the SIL Open Font License (OFL) Version 1.1 as presented, I am (you are) permitted to use the font in a print book (eBook) that you intend to sell. The license allows licensed fonts to be used, embedded, and redistributed freely, provided they are not sold by themselves.

Don’t Font Up

I believe the odds of being sued for misuse of fonts are minimal. I have not heard of Microsoft checking font usage for licensing. Other companies whose incomes may be based on font licensing may not be so lenient. So, forewarned is forearmed. The best time to address font licensing for your commercial ventures is before you are forced to address font licensing for your commercial ventures.

Chapter Conclusion

This chapter is an introduction to book marketing. Consider it an excursion into switching from your book creator's hat to your book business hat. This is not meant to be a comprehensive tutorial on book marketing and book production. It is meant to be an eye-opener, providing you with the insight to put on your business hat when planning a book for publication.

Chapter 21 – Starting A Side Hustle

Monetize this book's information - Basics of the Gig Economy

It's difficult to find a "niche" market that's not being serviced and then to service that market. Success can be found in broader markets by finding a unique spin on a service or product that people are already making money doing.

Save Your Customer's Time

I stated that using AI enhances one's output and essentially provides its users with more time, our most valuable commodity. In keeping with that idea, a side hustle that saves your customers time will (in my opinion) have a greater chance of success.

A friend asked me, why would he hire an individual to create comic book illustrations using AI, when he could run prompts into a text-to-art AI and do it himself.

There are multiple reasons to hire another person, beginning with talent and experience. You develop experience as you work with text-to-art AI's. It's a challenge to keep and direct the same character running through different panels. I suggested that if this became a real project for him, he'd be better served focusing on writing the narrative and dialog than the artwork. He remained unconvinced, but that's his inexperience.

The following lists provide ideas for monetizing the applications detailed in this book.

Book Marketing and Research Services

1. Amazon Market Research Service: Provide targeted research on book categories, including competing titles, audience size, and market gaps. Offer authors data-driven insights to help them decide whether their book idea has strong sales potential.
2. Amazon Sales Rank Reports: Use Amazon's Best Seller Rank calculators to estimate competitor sales volume. Deliver customized reports showing daily and monthly sales, helping authors set realistic expectations.
3. Formatting and Benchmarking Analysis: Analyze successful books in an author's niche to provide guidance on average page count, trim size, pricing, and review benchmarks. Present clear recommendations for positioning new titles competitively.
4. Print-on-Demand Cost Optimization: Compare KDP and IngramSpark printing costs to determine the most profitable publishing route. Provide detailed

breakdowns of printing expenses, royalty structures, and pricing strategies.

5. Children's Book Market Guidance: Specialize in helping children's book authors navigate challenges such as Amazon's page count minimums. Recommend best formats, trim sizes, and print/distribution solutions tailored to the children's market.
6. Done-for-You Research Package: Deliver complete research bundles including competitor analysis, sales rank calculations, formatting recommendations, and cost/profit breakdowns. Provide actionable insights so authors can publish with confidence.
7. Keyword and Category Optimization: Research and recommend the best keywords and Amazon categories to maximize discoverability. Help authors position their books where buyers are actively searching.
8. Competitive Title Reports: Create curated lists of 10–20 competing titles with detailed stats (sales rank, reviews, price, format). Provide authors with a snapshot of their competition and strategies to differentiate their book.
9. Profitability Forecasting: Build financial projections based on production costs, distribution options, and sales rank data. Show authors how different pricing models will affect their potential earnings.
10. Custom Market Feasibility Consultations: Offer one-on-one sessions where you walk authors through their book idea, analyze audience demand, and provide tailored recommendations for whether to move forward or pivot topics.

Creative Writing and Storytelling

1. Custom Content Creation: Use AI to generate detailed descriptions and narratives for websites, marketing materials, or creative projects. Offer specialized writing services to authors, game developers, or marketers needing unique, context-specific content.
2. Ghostwriting Fiction: Develop full novels, short stories, or series based on AI-generated outlines, turning basic ideas into complete manuscripts.
3. Writing Workshops and Courses: Offer online courses or workshops teaching writers how to use AI to develop story ideas, refine plots, and enhance character development.
4. Customized Story Creation: Provide personalized stories for private enjoyment, gifts, or special occasions using AI to generate unique plots based on customer preferences.
5. eBook Self-Publishing: Create and self-publish eBooks in popular genres or niches using AI to develop fiction content.
6. Scriptwriting for Media: Write scripts for films, plays, or video games, using AI to develop plot outlines and character descriptions.
7. Story Consultant Services: Offer AI-assisted story development services to writers or publishing agencies, helping overcome writer's block and expand existing plots.

8. Interactive and Serialized Fiction: Create interactive or serialized fiction for online platforms, using AI to outline plot branches or episodic content.
9. Fan Fiction and Alternative Endings: Generate and sell fan fiction or alternative endings for popular books, movies, or games, appealing to fan communities.
10. Collaborative Writing Projects: Organize collaborative writing projects with AI-generated frameworks, guiding the collaboration for cohesive storytelling.
11. AI-Assisted Writing Tools: Develop a platform offering AI-driven plot generation and advice for writers needing assistance in story development.
12. Thematic Content Generation: Provide services to create thematic content for events, such as custom greetings, invitations, or promotional content tailored to an event's theme.
13. Freelance Writing with Specific Emotional or Contextual Focus: Offer writing services specializing in specific emotional tones or moods, catering to content creators, marketers, or publishers.

Visual Art and Design

1. AI-Powered Artwork Creation: Transform text descriptions into artwork using AI tools. Cater to digital media, advertising, or clients needing unique art for personal or commercial use.

2. Personalized Gifts and Merchandise: Generate personalized poems, stories, or artwork for unique gifts or merchandise like T-shirts, mugs, or posters, especially for holidays or special occasions.

Education and Training

1. Educational Materials and Tutorials: Create educational content and tutorials on using AI for writing and art creation, including courses or workshops on effective prompt use for beginners and advanced users.
2. Educational Material Production: Develop comprehensive educational materials and curriculum guides for sale to educational institutions or online platforms.
3. Workshop and Seminar Content Preparation: Prepare content for workshops and seminars, providing fresh, reliable materials for professionals and educators.
4. Educational Materials for Different Learner Types: Create content that meets the needs of different learner types or age groups for engaging and age-appropriate study materials.
5. Financial Education and Tutorials: Teach financial chart analysis using AI through courses or ebooks.

Business and Professional Writing

1. Non-Fiction Writing Services: Develop non-fiction content from ideas to full drafts, catering to authors or professionals needing reports or guides.
2. E-Book Creation and Sales: Use AI to create non-fiction eBooks on various topics, editing and formatting for sale on platforms like Amazon Kindle.
3. Content Marketing: Create high-quality, researched articles for businesses and blogs, refining AI-generated drafts to meet professional standards.
4. Article Writing for Publications: Write articles for magazines, newspapers, and online publications, developing content that meets editorial standards.
5. Self-Help and How-To Guides: Create self-help and how-to guides on topics like personal development or technology using AI-generated content.
6. Freelance Academic Writing: Assist in creating structured outlines or sections of academic works, focusing on well-organized content.
7. Subscription Content Services: Offer a subscription service for regular, well-researched non-fiction content tailored to specific interests or industries.
8. Copywriting and Advertising: Develop persuasive advertising copy for small businesses or startups using AI to craft compelling pitches.
9. Content Personalization for Clients: Personalize content for individual users or customer bases, such as newsletters or user guides.

Digital Transformation and Automation

1. Document Digitization Services: Convert physical documents, photos of text, and handwritten notes into digital formats for businesses or individuals.
2. Data Entry Automation: Automate data entry tasks using AI to extract information from printed materials into structured digital formats.
3. Accessible Content Creation: Convert printed materials into digital text formats for text-to-speech tools for the visually impaired.
4. Translation Services: Offer translation services combining OCR with language translation capabilities for international documentation.
5. Archival Services: Digitize and archive legacy documents for libraries, academic institutions, or businesses.
6. Legal Document Handling: Convert legal documents, case files, or contracts into digital formats for law firms.
7. Content Repurposing: Transform printed marketing materials into digital content for online use.
8. eBook Creation: Convert handwritten manuscripts or printed texts into formatted eBooks for authors or publishers.
9. Educational Material Preparation: Digitize and prepare course materials for educational providers.

Financial Analysis and Advisory

1. Financial Analysis Services: Provide AI-based analysis of financial charts for investors or business owners.
2. Financial Blogging or Vlogging: Create content on financial education and investment strategies using AI analysis.
3. Subscription-Based Market Analysis: Offer regular AI-based analysis of financial markets through a subscription service.
4. Custom Financial Reports: Create reports analyzing historical data and predicting trends with AI assistance.
5. Automated Financial Advisory Services: Provide instant AI-generated analysis and advice on uploaded financial charts.
6. Data Visualization Services: Create financial charts and visualizations with AI-driven analysis.
7. Research Papers and Presentations: Prepare research papers, presentations, or reports requiring detailed chart analysis.
8. Real-time Financial Dashboard: Build a dashboard displaying real-time AI analysis of financial data.
9. AI-Powered Financial Planning Tools: Develop tools using AI for predictions and analysis based on personal financial data.

If you enjoy this book, please consider leaving a review.

https://www.amazon.com/review/create-review?&asin=B0DC5S85LV

Made in the USA
Monee, IL
04 November 2026

67382828R00095